Austria

Front cover: Hallstatt's Old Town
Right: Mozart statue, Salzburg

Maria Wörth Delightful village on Carinthia's most picturesque lake, the Wörthersee (page 77)

Tyrol The country's finest Alpine scenery: rugged peaks, verdant valleys, heart-warming villages, and a mecca for hikers and skiers (page 106)

The Hofburg Vienna's royal palace, brimming with Habsburg dynasty treasure (page 32)

Stift Melk The great Baroque monastery overlooking the scenic Danube valley (page 57)

Historic Salzburg Intended by its prince-archbishops to rival Rome (page 96)

Dachstein The spectacular south face can be ascended by cable car (page 71)

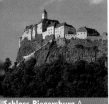

Schloss Riegersburg A fairy-tale castle atop a crag in southern Styria (page 54)

Schloss Schönbrunn Empress Maria Theresa's opulent palace and gardens in Vienna (page 46)

Innsbruck The Old Town with Emperor Maximilian's famous loggia, the Goldenes Dachl (page 106)

Hallstatt The exquisite little lakeside town is the jewel of the Salzkammergut (page 92)

A PERFECT TOUR

Day 1   Vienna

An early start is needed to fit in just the highlights of the Austrian capital. Begin at the Hofburg, the former centre of the Habsburg Empire. Gulaschmuseum (see page 150) is a great spot to lunch before a stroll around the Stephansdom and Vienna's medieval core. For dinner, sample Austrian cooking at Plachutta (see page 151), then dress up for a night at the Staatsoper.

Day 2   Viennese culture

Take the short U-Bahn ride to Schloss Schönnbrunn, the Habsburg's baroque masterpiece. After lunch, head back into the city centre to the MuseumsQuartier. There is a lot to see, so aim for what interests you. Finally, visit a *Heuriger* (wine tavern), perhaps Reinprecht (see page 150) in Grinzing.

Day 3   Graz

Just a two-hour drive on the A2 autobahn brings you to Graz. After a tour of the city centre with its mammoth armoury and baroque Schloss Eggenberg, it's time to head out into the countryside to visit two quintessentially Austrian sights. First up is the Österreichisches Freilichtmuseum (Austrian Open-Air Museum) with its examples of traditional rural architecture. A short drive west lies the Lipizzaner stud farm, which supplies Vienna's famous Riding School.

Day 4   Klagenfurt

The A2 autobahn continues southeast to pretty Klagenfurt, a 90-minute drive. After perusing the old city centre, take a pleasure boat along the Lendkanal, which links Klagenfurt to the wonderful Wörthersee, for some water sports fun or just a spot of sunbathing.

OF AUSTRIA

Day 6   Salzburg

Kick off with a hearty alpine breakfast in preparation for your ascent of the Mönchsberg and a tour of the Hohensalzburg. Lunch at the unmissable Café Tomaselli (see page 156) before strolling along the main Getreidegasse to see Mozart's birthplace. Cross the River Salzach for a scramble up the Kapuzinerberg, from where there are photogenic views of the left bank. End your day over some traditional fare and a few frothy tankards at the Die Weisse beer hall (see page 157).

Day 8   Innsbruck

A two-hour drive through the spectacular Alps and you are in Innsbruck, one of the unexpected highlights of any trip to Austria. The Alps seem to peer over the grand buildings of this enchanting city. Cable cars run up into the mountains for stupendous views.

Day 5   High Alps

Heading north from Klagenfurt, spend a lazy day admiring the widescreen alpine views from the famous Grossglockner Hochalpenstrasse, picnicking along the way. By early evening you should arrive in Salzburg, where dinner awaits at Magazin (see page 157).

Day 7   More Salzburg

Head south along the Salzach today, first to visit Schloss Hellbrunn, then to go underground at the former salt mine Salzwelten Salzburg and further south to the spectacular ice caves at Eisriesenwelt.

CONTENTS

Introduction 9

A Brief History 15

Where to Go 29
❶ *Numbered map references pinpoint the sights*

Vienna 29
*Inner City 29, The Hofburg 32, Ringstrasse 36,
Schloss Schönbrunn 46, Excursions 47*

Lower Austria 49
*Downstream from Vienna 50, Upstream from
Vienna 52, The Wachau and Stift Melk 55*

Burgenland 58
Eisenstadt 59, Neusiedler See 60

Styria 60
*Graz 61, Excursions from Graz 65, Styrian vineyards
and spas 66, Mariazell 68, Leoben 69, Dachstein 71*

Carinthia and East Tyrol 72
*Klagenfurt 72, Wörthersee 75, Villach and Ossiacher
See 79, Drau Valley 81, East Tyrol 83*

Upper Austria 84
Linz 84, Steyr 87, The Mühlviertel 88

The Salzkammergut 88
*Bad Ischl 89, Wolfgangsee and Mondsee 90,
Hallstatt 92, Bad Aussee 94*

Salzburg and Salzburger Land 95
*Salzburg 96, Along the Salzach 100, Badgastein 102,
The Pinzgau 102, Grossglockner 104*

Tyrol 106
*Innsbruck 106, Brenner Pass 110, Achensee and
Zillertal 113, Seefeld 115, Arlberg 118*

Vorarlberg 120
Bregenz 121, Bregenzerwald 123, Feldkirch 124

What to Do 127
Active Pursuits 127
Shopping 133
Entertainment 135
Children's Austria 139

Eating Out 141

A–Z Travel Tips 159

Hotels 181

Index 189

Features

Country of Music 12
The Unfortunate Archduke 23
Sissi 33
Jugendstil 42
Richard Lionheart 57
Friedensreich Hundertwasser 64
The Klagenfurt Lindwurm 73
The Salzburg Festival 98
Andreas Hofer 109
South Tyrol/Alto Adige 111
Ötzi 117
Spas 132
Das Kaffeehaus 147

INTRODUCTION

This prosperous little Alpine republic and its capital – Vienna – present an alluring image to the outside world. Its scenic beauties draw visitors here in their millions in summer and winter, while millions more revel in its unsurpassed cultural heritage. Its charm is legendary, its inhabitants welcoming, its cuisine heartily filling. In many ways it seems a model country, a parliamentary democracy and member of the European Union whose geographical location and neutral status has made it a bridge between East and West. An ancient Latin epithet *Felix Austria* ('O Happy Austria!') would seem to apply today as much as when it was coined several hundred years ago. But before reaching this enviable state, the country was beset by crises of identity and a history more turbulent than most.

The Country

Landlocked Austria stretches for some 700km (440 miles) between two great lakes, Bodensee (Lake Constance) in the west, and Neusiedlersee in the east. Lake Constance is shared with two neighbours, Switzerland and Germany; Neusiedlersee with Hungary. Two-thirds of the country is mountainous. The Northern Limestone Alps form the boundary with Bavaria, while the centre of the country is dominated by a chain of imposing peaks including the country's highest summit, the Grossglockner (3,798m/12,46ft). In the south, the jagged outline of the Southern Limestone Alps mark the frontier with northeast Italy and Slovenia. Far from being impenetrable, in most places the mountains are threaded by river valleys and by numerous passes such as the Brenner which have been used since prehistoric times. The formidable

The village of Weyregg am Attersee in Upper Austria

Austria is famous for its beautiful Alpine scenery

barrier of the central Alps has been overcome in recent times by the construction of the Grossglockner High Alpine Road and by rail and motorway tunnels. Lowland Austria consists of the lands on either side of the great water highway of the Danube; to the north these rise to rounded wooded summits along the border with the Czech Republic, while the southeastern part of the country opens out towards the plains of Hungary and southern Slovakia.

Austria is not rich in natural resources, though mineral ores and salt have been mined in the mountains since early times and there is an important oilfield northeast of Vienna. Most energy is supplied by hydroelectric power. Only the lowlands support large-scale cultivation, with vineyards and orchards forming wonderful patterns in southern Styria, Burgenland and Lower Austria. Having lived through hard times, the country underwent a minor economic miracle in the late 20th century, largely thanks to the development of the service sector and to the continuing growth of the mainstay of its economy – tourism.

Regions
Austria is a federal republic of nine provinces (Bundesländer) including Vienna, each with its own government and

legislature. Until quite recently, the majority of the country's inhabitants would have described themselves as Tyroleans, Salzburgers, Styrians and so on rather than as Austrians. Local loyalties are strong mainly because historically the provinces led largely independent lives and developed distinct identities of their own. Today, each *Land* (Region) offers visitors its particular version of Austrian hospitality and its own enticing range of attractions and activities. Deeply proud of its folk traditions, ever-popular Tyrol has more than its fair share of spectacular Alpine scenery as well as heaps of enchanting old villages and towns. The provinces of Lower and Upper Austria are linked by the Danube, its waters plied by pleasure steamers, its banks carpeted with vineyards while medieval castles and great abbeys survey the scene. Not a province in its own right, the Salzkammergut with its glorious lakes and mountains is shared between Upper Austria, Salzburger Land and Styria. The jewel of Salzburger Land is of course its historically intriguing capital, Salzburg itself, one of Europe's great city-break destinations. Styria's chief city, ancient and characterful Graz, is the gateway to the 'Styrian Tuscany', a surprisingly delightful region of rolling hills and vineyards which fully merits its name. The warm-water lakes of southern Carinthia have long been a favourite with Austrian holiday-makers, while to the north, the province is linked to neighbouring Salzburger Land by the Grossglockner Road, the main route into the snowcapped Hohe Tauern range, now a National Park. Wonderfully scenic lakes characterise Austria's smallest provinces. To the east of Vienna, on the border with Hungary, the gentle countryside of the Burgenland stretches out around the shallow Neusiedlersee, a water sports paradise as well

A wooded land

Austria is one of the most wooded countries in Europe, with more than a third of its surface covered in forest, most of it coniferous.

as an internationally important nature reserve. In the far west, beyond the mountain barrier of the Arlberg, the province of Vorarlberg shares much with Switzerland including the ocean-like Lake Constance (of which Bavaria has its tiny bit, too).

In the past, the inhabitants of the provinces lived on the land or in small towns and no more looked to Vienna than did the citizens of other parts of the Empire. In any case, the imperial capital had become ever more cosmopolitan. Many of the aristocrats clustering around the Imperial court had roots in Poland, Italy, Hungary and in the Czech provinces of Bohemia and Moravia. In the 19th century, economic expansion was largely financed by Jewish capital and industry depended on a workforce drawn from all quarters of the Empire; by 1900 almost a quarter of the population was Czech by origin. Such variety was not characteristic of most provincial places, which clung to their Germanic character and nurtured their traditions, many of which remain very much alive today. Vienna by contrast was and is a centre of innovation and experiment in many spheres, and, with a population of around 1.7 million

Country of Music

Austria is a supremely musical nation, and Vienna's claim to be the world capital of music is no exaggeration. No other country has nurtured so many composers, from Haydn, Mozart and Beethoven to Schubert, the Strausses, Bruckner and Mahler, and on to the masters of atonality, Schönberg, Webern and Berg. And in few other cities is classical music and opera taken so seriously by the general population, who have an enviable choice of world-class orchestras and who worship in one of the world's great temples to music, the Staatsoper. The provinces also maintain the highest of musical standards, with a dazzling calendar of festivals and events of which the world-famous Salzburg Festspiele is a truly unique spectacle.

remains something of an anomaly in this small country of just under 8.4 million. It remains a great centre of European culture and a magnet for visitors from all over the world.

Culture

At a European crossroads, Austria has always been open to influences from its neighbours, above all from Germany and Italy. The Imperial court and a powerful Church acted as patrons at various points in history, while Vienna has witnessed more than one period of extraordinary creative endeavour in the arts.

As elsewhere, churches are a great repository of art and architecture. Nearly every parish church in Austria is of some interest, if not for architectural features from the Romanesque period, then for artwork and embellishment from the Gothic or Renaissance and above all from the Baroque era. St Stephen's in Vienna is one of the greatest of all medieval cathedrals, with furnishings of superlative quality. Unsurprisingly in a country with abundant timber supplies, woodcarving flourished in the late Middle Ages. Its most gifted exponent was the Tyrolean Michael Pacher (c.1435–98), responsible for marvellous altarpieces, including those made for the parish churches at St Wolfgang and Heiligenblut. The impact of the Italian Renaissance took time to be felt in Austria, but can be seen in splendid courtyard palaces such as Spittal's Schloss Porcia and above all in the extravagant tomb built for himself in Innsbruck by

Classical music on a Viennese street

The monumental Stift Melk

Emperor Maximilian I. The greatest project of this era was the attempt by successive Archbishops of Salzburg to rebuild their city as a challenger to Rome.

In the late 17th and early 18th century, the Counter-Reformation found the perfect vehicle for its blend of mysticism and theatricality in the playful elegance of the Baroque style, which reached its zenith in Austria and remains one of the country's greatest attractions. In the building boom that followed the raising of the Turkish siege of Vienna in 1682, numerous new churches were erected and older ones remodelled. In the countryside, great medieval abbeys like Melk and St Florian were transformed into what have been called 'monuments of militant Catholicism', and few parish churches escaped a Baroque makeover. In Vienna, the summit of extravagance was reached in the magnificent domed Karlskirche, the masterpiece of Johann Bernhard Fischer von Erlach (1656–1723), as well as in the Belvedere palace and gardens built for the conqueror of the Turks, Prince Eugene of Savoy.

Baroque was a hard act to beat, but Austrian architects later led the way in the international Art Nouveau movement, known in the German-speaking world as Jugendstil, for which Vienna set the standard for the rest of central Europe (see page 42).

A BRIEF HISTORY

Much of the history of Austria deals with lands well beyond the boundaries of today's little Alpine republic. Not so long ago the country now called Austria was the core of a vast empire covering much of Central Europe. In more recent times the period when Austria was swallowed up by the Third Reich and simply ceased to exist as an independent nation still lives in the memory. Re-established after the calamities of World War II, the country has subsequently enjoyed six decades of peaceful evolution and integration into a wider Europe. However, the contrast between the Austria of today and the country it has been in the past means that history weighs more heavily on Austrians than on many other peoples.

Before Austria

Fascinating traces of the country's early inhabitants remain in places like Hallstatt, where Illyrians and Celts mined salt and which gave its name to an Iron Age culture that flourished in central Europe between 800 and 400BC. Famous Ötzi, the 'Man in the Ice' is older still, having met his violent end high in the Tyrolean Alps thousands of years before (see page 117). The most powerful Celtic kingdom was that of the Norici, which, as Noricum, became part of the Roman Empire in 15BC. Roman expansion was halted on

A relic from the Celtic past

A depiction of the battle of Lechfeld

the Danube, which formed the fortified frontier of the Empire for hundreds of years. Vindobona, today's Vienna, was one of many settlements guarding the border, while Carnuntum not far to the east, was one of the largest Roman towns in Central Europe, with a population of 70,000. Pressure from Germanic tribes was a constant threat to Roman rule, though their final withdrawal in the 5th century came with the onslaught of Attila the Hun and his armies. For hundreds of years, along with much of the rest of Europe, the area of present-day Austria was the subject of complex patterns of migration and temporary rule by Ostrogoths, Langobards, Avars and Slavs.

The Ostmark

By the 8th century, the chaotic era of the great migrations had more or less come to an end, succeeded by a more settled period in which Germanic peoples consolidated their power and began a steady expansion eastwards. At the expense of the Slavs, the Bavarians pushed south into Carinthia as well as east along the Danube to the line of the River Enns. They brought Christianity with them, founding an archbishopric at Salzburg in 798. To protect the newly settled areas, a system of marcher realms was set up, including the Ostmark (Eastern Marches), the area forming today's Upper and Lower Austria. This failed to withstand the onrush of pagan Hungarian warriors, who terrorised the region for the first half of the 10th century, but were decisively defeated by the German army of Otto I at the great battle of the Lechfeld in 955. Otto made use of this success to become Holy Roman Emperor, a title which eventually passed to the Habsburgs and was only consigned to the dustbin of history in 1806.

In 976, the German Count Leopold of Babenberg was given control of the re-established Ostmark, and it was under his rule that the name Ostarrichi was first recorded, the forerunner of today's Österreich/Austria. During the Babenbergs' 300-year rule, they extended their realm eastwards along the Danube, bringing in German peasants to settle the land, founding great monasteries such as Melk and Klosterneuburg and finally establishing themselves in Vienna, which they made their capital in 1150. But Babenberg Austria was still only the kernel of what was to become a far larger state; the archbishopric of Salzburg was part of Bavaria, and remained so until modern times; Tyrol remained a patchwork of tiny fiefdoms until it was united in the 12th century; Carinthia was an independent dukedom; and Vorarlberg looked towards what was to become Switzerland. But Styria was acquired in 1192, filling the coffers of state with the profits from its great iron mine at Erzberg. When the Babenbergs died out in 1246, the Austrian nobility invited King Ottakar II of Bohemia to become their ruler. The energetic Ottakar embarked on a vigorous programme of expansion, and at one point seemed to be on the verge of establishing a realm reaching from the Baltic to the Adriatic, a forerunner of the later Empire. But at the battle of Dürnkrut near Vienna in 1278, Ottakar was defeated and killed by the newly elected King of Germany, Rudolf of Habsburg.

Enter the Habsburgs

The Habsburgs took their name from their castle in what is now Switzerland, the 'Habichtsburg' (Hawk Fortress). It was their relative insignificance that made Rudolf a suitable candidate for kingship in the eyes of the other German princes, who thought it would be easy to manipulate him. But Rudolf set the Habsburgs on a course which would elevate them from minor princelings to the rulers of a mighty domain with a God-given mission to dominate Christendom. Their fortunes fluctuated: in the course of the 14th century they acquired Carinthia, Tyrol, Istria and parts of Vorarlberg, but met with strong resistance from the emerging Swiss Confederation.

The Habsburgs were of course quite happy to wage war when they saw fit, but their greatest acquisitions, like Spain and Burgundy, were indeed engineered by shrewd marriage alliances with other dynasties. By the time Charles V was crowned Holy Roman Emperor in 1520, their inheritance was so vast and unwieldy that he subdivided it; while he continued to rule over Spain and the Netherlands, his brother Ferdinand was given responsibility for the Austrian lands, and it was this branch of the Habsburgs that now faced new threats.

Protestants and Ottomans

In the course of the early 16th century Protestantism had spread over much of Austria, with many converts among the nobility, the townsfolk and the mining communities. With their sense of a divine mission, the Habsburgs were bound to oppose such heresy, though they were often forced into compromise because of the need to deal with the even greater menace posed by the powerful armies of the Ottoman Empire. Advancing northwards from their Balkan base, in 1526 the Turks smashed a Christian army at Mohács in southern Hungary. In the course of the battle, Louis, King of Hungary and Bohemia, was killed, his crown passing to Ferdinand. At great cost, Ferdinand succeeded in halting the Ottoman advance; a month-long siege of Vienna in 1529 ended in a Turkish retreat to their headquarters at Budapest, but the scene was set for a century and a half of tension and con-

Portrait of Archduke Rudolf Habsburg

flict, with lines of Habsburg and Ottoman forces facing one another across a devastated landscape.

The Protestant/Catholic conflict came to a head in the early 17th century. In Bohemia (a Habsburg possession since 1526), many members of the local aristocracy had embraced the new faith (Protestantism), and were furious at Habsburg attempts to restrict religious freedom. In 1618, in a violent gesture of defiance, a group of them threw a pair of Imperial councillors from the windows of Prague Castle. This lit the blue touchpaper for the Thirty Years War, a conflict that wrecked much of Germany and Bohemia though Austria itself remained largely spared. Early Habsburg successes were reversed when France and Sweden entered the war, and hopes of re-Catholicising swathes of Europe were given up at the 1648 Treaty of Westphalia which brought hostilities to a close. But peace left the Habsburgs free to impose their will on their own possessions. An alliance of Dynasty, Church and higher aristocracy forced through the Counter-Reformation; Protestants unwilling to convert were expelled, but a powerful incentive to turn to true belief was provided by the widespread construction and lavish decoration of countless churches in the new Baroque style, a major contribution to the country's architectural heritage.

Turkish delights

The Turkish siege of Vienna, led by Kara Mustafa, left a couple of culinary legacies. The coffee beans discovered in their abandoned encampment led to the setting up of the first coffee houses in the city. Victory over a Muslim army was celebrated by the baking of Kipfel, the crescent-shaped pastries better known in French and English as croissants.

In 1683 the Turks made a second and more determined attempt to capture Vienna. Grand Vizier Kara Mustafa advanced on the city with a quarter of a million troops, subjecting it to a two-month siege, which was only lifted when a combined Imperial and Polish army attacked from the Kahlenberg heights. This defeat marked the beginning of the end of the Turkish threat and their forces were hurled back into the Balkans. The Habsburgs were well served by their great commander, Paris-born Prince Eugene of Savoy, who won his greatest victory over the Ottoman army at Zenta in 1697 and went on to build himself one of Vienna's finest palaces, the Belvedere.

Enlightened Rule

In the 18th century the Habsburg court was one of the most glittering in Europe, and Vienna one of the most cosmopolitan of cities. The capital's face continued to be beautified by the building of great Baroque churches and palaces, while its cultural life was enriched by the presence of artists, composers

Statue of Prince Eugene of Savoy on Heldenplatz, Vienna

and craftsmen drawn from all over the continent. The era is inextricably linked with Empress Maria Theresa (1740–80) and her son, Joseph II (1780–90). Both strove to modernise the country: Maria Theresa created a class of conscientious civil servants and introduced compulsory schooling for children throughout the empire; Joseph was the archetypal ruler of the period of the Enlightenment, bringing in reforms such as the abolition of serfdom and the dissolution of monasteries, as well as freeing Jews and Protestants from many of the restrictions previously imposed on them. But progress stalled, first in the face of entrenched interests, then because of the threat posed by Revolutionary France, whose zealots had executed Marie Antoinette, Louis XIV's Habsburg wife.

Restoration and Revolution

Austria's role in Napoleon's defeat was not a particularly glorious one, but the country's capital nevertheless played host to the great Congress of Vienna of 1815, in which the victorious powers redrew the map of Europe in an attempt to inoculate the continent against any renewed outbreak of revolution. Having given up the title of Holy Roman Emperor in 1806, Franz I now found himself compensated for the loss of the Austrian Netherlands

The domes of Artstetten Castle

with Salzburg and with new acquisitions in northern Italy. The monarchy's leading figure was the Chancellor, Prince Metternich, who instituted an authoritarian regime hostile to all forms of dissent, supported by a notoriously repressive secret police force and an army of informers. By 1848 resentment had reached such a pitch that news of the outbreak of revolution in Paris sparked off risings in Vienna and full-scale rebellion in Budapest and Prague. The government toyed with ideas of a new constitutional settlement, but the uprisings were eventually put down and an 18-year-old Emperor, Franz Joseph I, mounted the throne with one aim in mind, the maintenance of his dynasty's imperial heritage.

Domkirche St. Stephan zu Wien

Einzelkarte / Single Ticket

Nord Turm

Aufzug zur Pummerin
Lift to the Pummerin

EUR 5,00   Nr. 3308888

1 Erwachsener

1 Adult

www.stephanskirche.at & www.domshop-wien.at
Kirchenmeisteramt St. Stephan, Stephansplatz 3, 1010 Wien

Stephansdom
Wien

Franz Joseph

'I have been spared nothing', was Franz Joseph's sad comment on his reign and on his personal life. Wars in 1859 and 1866 deprived his Empire of much of northern Italy and ended any Austrian influence on a rapidly unifying Germany. Worse still, his restless Hungarian subjects demanded, and got the *Ausgleich* (Compromise), which transformed the Empire into the Dual Monarchy. Austria and Hungary were now virtually separate states, linked only in the person of the monarch, though foreign affairs and the army remained under the control of Vienna. A rising tide of nationalism among the Empire's dozen or more peoples made government more and more difficult, not least because the reforms necessary to adapt the country to a rapidly changing, industrialising world were only granted with great reluctance. But most Austrians remained loyal to the Emperor, not least out of sympathy for the tragedies that beset him. In 1867 his brother Maximilian was executed, and in 1889 his son and heir, Rudolph, shot his mistress and then himself at his hunting lodge at Mayerling. A further devastating blow came in 1898 with the murder of his beloved wife Sissi at the hands of an anarchist, then, in

The Unfortunate Archduke

Shunned by the Imperial court because he had married beneath him (a mere countess!), Archduke Franz Ferdinand was nevertheless expected to succeed Emperor Franz Joseph on the aged ruler's death. The Archduke's plans for modernising the monarchy, in particular his wish to allow Slav subjects a greater role in its governance, came to nothing when he, together with his much-loved wife Sophie, fell to a Serbian assassin's bullet as he drove through the streets of Sarajevo. Even in death, Imperial protocol refused the couple burial together in Vienna's Hofburg, and their tombs are in Artstetten Castle.

June 1914, the assassination of Archduke Franz Ferdinand, his nephew and heir to the throne, unleashed a war the Emperor had long dreaded.

The First Republic

After a reign lasting 60 years, Franz Joseph died in 1916; his young and inexperienced successor, Karl I, tried vainly to make peace and hold the now disintegrating Empire together. But the various nationalities of the Empire went their own way, carving new states like Czechoslovakia and Yugoslavia out of its corpse. Forbidden by the victorious Allies to unite with Germany, Austria's German-speakers found themselves in a tiny state consisting of 'what no one else wanted', the Empire's Alpine and Danubian provinces. The Imperial capital, Vienna, was now grotesquely oversized for its role, a head with an attenuated body. Emperor Karl went into exile on the Portuguese island of Madeira, and a democratic republic was declared.

From the start it was plagued by conflict, with well-armed groups on both Right and Left attempting to gain ascendancy, and a Socialist Vienna viewed with hostility by the conservative provinces. In 1933 the Right under Chancellor Dollfuss seized its chance, establishing a corporate regime on the model of Mussolini's Fascist Italy. In 1934 a workers' rising was easily smashed by police and army, who used artillery to bombard Vienna's showpiece public housing. Later that year, a rising by Austria's Nazis also failed, though they succeeded in killing the unfortunate Dollfuss. His successor, Kurt Schuschnigg, also tried to keep Austria out of the Third Reich, but, browbeaten by Hitler, resigned on 11 March 1938. On 12 March, *heiled* by ecstatic crowds, German troops marched in, accompanied by their triumphant, Austrian-born Führer, who proclaimed *Anschluss* with the Reich.

Occupation and War

Hitler had hated Habsburg Austria and its cosmopolitan capital where Germans seemed outnumbered by Jews and other 'inferior races', and he now relished the opportunity to dismember the country. The name 'Austria' disappeared, replaced by the historic term 'Ostmark' with all its implications of a barrier against the menacing East. Even this was abolished in 1942, leaving the Austrian provinces simply as units of 'Greater Germany'. The euphoria which many had felt at the *Anschluss* soon gave way to resentment at German dominance, then as the war

German troops on the Ringstrasse in 1938

began to go badly, to widespread fear and anxiety. Active resistance was difficult, if not impossible, and in any case most Austrians 'did their duty', serving in the Wehrmacht, and, in disproportionately large numbers, in the SS and other Nazi formations.

In 1943, the western Allies and the Soviet Union agreed that the country, characterised as 'Hitler's first victim', albeit with its share of war guilt, was to be re-established in its pre-*Anschluss* boundaries. On 16 April 1945, Vienna was 'liberated' by the Soviet army, and Austria, like Germany, was subsequently divided into four occupation zones: American, British, French and Soviet.

The latest news in a Vienna café

Post-War Austria and Into the 21st Century

Four-power occupation lasted until 1955, when the 'State Treaty' was signed, restoring full independence on condition of Austria's permanent neutrality on the Swiss model. After the decade of hardship that followed the war, the economy now grew rapidly, and by the 1970s many could agree with Pope Paul VI that their country was indeed an 'island of the blessed'. Chancellor Bruno Kreisky led the country on a path of liberal reform as well as focusing on a range of important international issues. But Austrian complacency was shaken in the 1980s when their president, Kurt Waldheim, was revealed to have deliberately kept quiet about his wartime role as a Wehrmacht officer. Many Austrians resented the way in which the country was subsequently cold-shouldered by the international community. The maverick politician, Jörg Haider, was able to manipulate such resentments to the advantage of his right-wing Freedom Party, which in 2000 entered a coalition government, though the challenges of office soon caused it to self-destruct. The consensus politics which characterised the whole post-war era were shaken by the Haider episode, and subsequent governments have had to perform adroit balancing acts faced with issues such as immigration and the 'War on Terror'. More recently, the world's 12th-richest country has weathered the economic storm better than most in the region and remains one of Europe's more stable economies.

Historical Highlights

c.3300BC Bronze Age mountain man Ötzi murdered.

800–400BC Flourishing Hallstatt Culture.

15BC–AD433 Austria south of the Danube under Roman rule.

4th–9th centuries Barbarian invasions.

798 Archbishopric of Salzburg founded.

976–1246 Rule of Babenberg dynasty.

1278 Duke Rudolf inaugurates six centuries of Habsburg rule.

1493–1519 Maximilian I, Holy Roman Emperor, extends Habsburg rule to Burgundy, the Netherlands and Spain.

1526 Hungary becomes a Habsburg possession.

1529 First Turkish siege of Vienna.

1618–48 The Thirty Years War.

1683 Second Turkish siege of Vienna ends with rout of the Ottoman army. Austrian rule extended far into the Balkans.

1740–90 Enlightened rule of Maria Theresa and her son Joseph II.

1792–1815 Intermittent war with France. Andreas Hofer leads popular revolt against the French in Tyrol.

1848 Emperor Franz Joseph begins 60-year rule.

1866 Defeat to Prussia excludes Austria from influence in Germany.

1867 The *Ausgleich* (Compromise) weakens the Empire.

1914 Assassination of Archduke Franz Ferdinand in Sarajevo.

1918 Collapse of Austria-Hungary, end of Habsburg rule and proclamation of the Austrian Republic.

1934 Chancellor Dollfuss assassinated by Nazis.

1938 The *Anschluss* incorporates Austria into Hitler's Germany.

1945 'Liberation' by Allies and re-establishment of Republic.

1955 The 'State Treaty' commits Austria to neutrality.

1995 Austria joins the European Union.

2000 Far right Freedom Party enters government for first time.

2007 Social Democrat-led coalition government inaugurated.

2012 The gravestone of Adolf Hitler's parents removed from village of Leonding to prevent use as neo-Nazi pilgrimage site.

WHERE TO GO

VIENNA

One of the world's great cities, **Vienna ❶** never fails to charm its visitors, not only with an incomparable heritage of Habsburg history, art and architecture, beauty and musicality, but with that untranslatable quality of *Gemütlichkeit*, a mixture of cosiness and amiable hospitality, best experienced in a traditional coffee house or wine tavern. Now with a population of around 1.7 million, fewer than when it was the centre of a great empire, Vienna is large enough to be a true metropolis but small enough to be easily understood and explored. The city is laid out at the point where the Danube flows through the gap between the Alps to the west and the Carpathians to the east. In the shape of the Wienerwald (Vienna Woods), the easternmost foothills of the Alps descend through forests and vineyards to the very edge of the city, where old wine villages like Grinzing have kept their rustic character. Within the Ringstrasse, the great semi-circular boulevard laid out in the 19th century, the old core of the city is compact enough to be explored on foot. The famous Hofburg, the rambling city palace of the Habsburgs, is matched by its out-of-town equivalent Schloss Schönbrunn, Vienna's glorious answer to Versailles.

Inner City

At the meeting point of Vienna's two most important shopping streets (Kärntnerstrasse and Graben), and served by two U-Bahn (Underground) lines, **Stephansplatz** makes an excellent starting point for an exploration of the Inner City. The square is dominated by Vienna's number one attraction, the

Nighttime view over central Vienna

great mass of the much-loved **Stephansdom** Ⓐ (St Stephen's Cathedral; guided tour in English daily 3.45pm; towers daily 9am–5.30pm; charge), which has withstood Turkish sieges and French bombardment, to say nothing of the bombing and shelling of World War II. Begun in 1365, it's a masterpiece of Gothic architecture, though its builder incorporated the two towers of its Romanesque predecessor, which, nicknamed *Heidentürme* (Heathen Towers), now flank the main portal. Of the two Gothic towers planned, one (to the north) was never completed; capped with a Renaissance cupola, it remains a stump housing the largest bell in Austria, the Pummerin or 'boomer'. The south tower, the Stephansturm, known familiarly to Viennese as *Steffl*, soars to a height of 137m (449ft); with fabulous views over the city and its surroundings, it was used as an observation post during the Turkish siege of 1683. The cathedral's immensely high roof with the Habsburg double eagle picked out in colourful tiles has been meticulously restored after destruction in World War II. The Gothic majesty of the interior has in no way been diminished by the insertion of Baroque altarpieces, and many original features remain, among them the charming pulpit carved by a sculptor who portrayed himself peering out through a window.

Sacher's tart

One of Vienna's most renowned confections, the chocolate *Sachertorte*, can be sampled on its home ground just off Kärntnerstrasse, at the Café Sacher in Philharmonikerstrasse.

Around Stephansplatz

Once protected by walls and moats, the area to the north of Stephansplatz was the site of Roman Vindobona and of early medieval Vienna. With many a Baroque church and aristocratic palace, its streets and squares are a delight to explore. A passageway by the east end of the Cathedral leads to narrow Domgasse and the **Mozarthaus** (daily 10am–7pm; charge). Mozart lived here from 1784 to 1787, one of his most productive periods, during which he composed his *Marriage of Figaro*. In 2006 the museum was completely redesigned to mark the 250th anniversary of Mozart's birth.

The roof of the Stephansdom

The old city's watery defences are recalled in the name of the broad, traffic-free street leading northwestwards from Stephansplatz; lined with fine buildings of various dates, most of which now house elegant shops and cafés, the **Graben** (moat) has long been a place to see and be seen. At its centre stands the elaborate Baroque **Pestsäule**, one of many erected all over Austria to mark the end of outbreaks of the plague. In Dorotheergasse, the **Jüdisches Museum** (Sun–Fri 10am–6pm; charge) traces the history of Vienna's Jewish community from its beginnings in the Middle Ages to its end under Nazi rule. In a little square, the **Peterskirche** has one of the loveliest interiors of all Vienna's Baroque churches.

Running south from Stephansplatz, the pedestrianised **Kärntnerstrassse** is one of the city's busiest and most important streets, lined like the Graben with up-market shops. It leads to the huge neo-Renaissance **Staatsoper (tours in English 2pm, 3pm)**, one of the world's great opera houses.

A portrait of Empress
Elisabeth, or 'Sissi'

Completed in 1869, the opera was one of the first of the monumental edifices to grace the Ringstrasse, and ever since has been dear to the heart of the Viennese, one of the world's more critical audiences.

The Hofburg

For centuries the **Hofburg** Ⓑ was the Habsburg dynasty's main home. This sprawling palace in a variety of architectural styles is now the country's principal monument to their memory, with an assortment of interiors and museums to keep the keen visitor occupied for days. It is also the official residence of the President. Its fortifications have long since given way to gardens and open spaces liberally dotted with heroic statuary. Next to the Opera, the **Burggarten** is graced by a vast and elegant Jugendstil glasshouse, part of which is given over to a butterfly garden, part to an excellent café. Guarded by the monumental Burgtor gateway, the rather bleak **Heldenplatz** (Heroes' Square) links the Ringstrasse to the Hofburg as well as providing a public thoroughfare through the palace to the Inner City. Beyond, the **Volksgarten** (People's Park) was laid out in formal, French style in 1823 as the city's first public park. A Greek temple forms its centrepiece, while to one side is a Jugendstil memorial to 'Sissi'.

If the Habsburg regime had survived, most of the Volksgarten would have been replaced by a new wing of the palace, planned to complete the enclosure of Heldenplatz begun by the construction of the **Neue Burg**. Completed in 1913, this 'New Castle' in heavy neo-Renaissance style now houses several first-rate museums (Wed–Mon 10am–6pm; combined charge): the **Museum für Völkerkunde** (Ethnology) has extraordinary objects from Benin as well as the Captain Cook collection of South Seas artefacts; the **Ephesus Museum** brings together superb Ancient Greek finds excavated by Austrian archaeologists; the **Sammlung alter Musikinstrumenten** displays the world's finest array of musical instruments from the Renaissance; while the arms and armour on show in the **Hofjagd und Rüstkammer** are almost without equal in Europe.

To the north of the Heldenplatz is the **Alte Burg** (Old Castle), the original core of the palace complex. The private quarters of the Imperial family, the **Kaiserappartements** (daily 9am–5.30pm, July, Aug until 6pm; charge), are lavish enough, though not quite in the same league as those at

Sissi

Aged only sixteen when she married Emperor Franz Joseph in 1854, the Bavarian princess Elisabeth found stuffy court life unbearably oppressive, not least because of the presence of her watchful mother-in-law, Archduchess Sophie. She was a fitness freak before her time, loved riding, and was at her happiest in Hungary with its traditions of skilful horsemanship. Often separated from her tolerant and loving husband by his devotion to affairs of state, her restless spirit found relief in travel, and it was on a trip to Switzerland in 1898 that she was stabbed to death by an Italian anarchist. A Sissi cult lives on in romantic films, a musical and in many a souvenir.

Members of the Vienna Boys' Choir

Schönbrunn; the main attraction here is the **Sissimuseum**, devoted to the cult of Franz Joseph's tragic consort. The Gothic **Burgkapelle** (Palace Chapel; June–Sept Mon–Thur 11am–3pm, Fri 11am, 1pm; charge) is the home of the world-famous Vienna Boys' Choir, who regularly sing at Sunday Mass. The immensely long and weighty past of the dynasty is perhaps most strongly felt in the **Schatzkammer** **C** (Imperial Treasury; Wed–Mon 9am–5.30pm; charge). Among the crown jewels, ceremonial robes and regalia, and imperial insignia attesting to the power, prestige and glory of the monarchy and its predecessors, the outstanding item is the Imperial Crown of the Holy Roman Empire, sometimes held to have been made for Charlemagne himself. There are also some preposterous holy relics, including the lance with which the Roman soldier is supposed to have pierced Christ's side.

Many visitors come to the Hofburg for the sole purpose of admiring the snow-white Lipizzaner horses of the **Spanish**

Riding School being put through their paces in the spacious interior of the **Winterreitschule**, a Baroque masterpiece created by the architect Josef Emanuel Fischer von Erlach. Horses perform in the arena throughout the year, except in July and August (Tue–Sun 9am–4pm; charge; visit www.srs.at for details of performances and training sessions).

To the south of the Stallburg, Josefsplatz gives access to the National Library, the centrepiece of which is the gorgeous Baroque **Prunksaal** (Great Hall; Tue–Wed, Fri–Sun 10am–6pm, Thur 10am–9pm; charge). Designed by Fischer von Erlach, it's the largest such room in Europe, lavishly decorated and rising through two storeys to an oval dome. In the crypt of the adjacent **Augustinerkirche**, the Habsburgs' wedding church, silver urns contain the hearts and entrails of members of the dynasty. The crypt can only be seen by appointment, but more substantial Habsburg remains, or at least the tombs containing them, can be visited in the famous **Kaisergruft** (Imperial Burial Vault; daily 10am–6pm; charge) in the Kapuzinerkirche a short walk north in Neuer Markt. The most elaborate tomb is Empress Maria Theresa's, the most recent that of Empress Zita, widow of the last Emperor Karl I, who died in 1989.

Situated beyond the Augustinerkirche, overlooking the rear of the Opera, the **Albertina** (Mon, Tue, Thur–Sun 10am–6pm, Wed until 9pm; charge) is home to the world's largest and most important collection of graphic art. The million-plus items include works by

Spanish Riding School equipment

virtually every artist of note, from the Old Masters to the likes of Klimt and Schiele.

The Ringstrasse

In 1859, Franz Joseph signed the order for the razing of the city defences, and for their replacement by the 4km (2.5-mile) -long, 60m (200ft) -wide Ringstrasse. The 'Ring' soon became the setting for a generation of monumental public buildings as well as the best address in town for shops and luxury apartments. In contrast to the Inner City, dominated by the Hofburg and by churches and aristocratic palaces, its museums, educational institutions, stock exchange and administrative buildings symbolised the growing power and influence of the rising, liberally minded middle classes, many of them of Jewish origin. The best way of getting an overall impression of this magnificent thoroughfare is to take the tram from one end to the other, then to visit those sections or individual buildings of most interest.

Twin Museums

Together with the Natural History Museum, Vienna's **Kunsthistorisches Museum** **D** (Art Historical Museum; Tue–Sun 10am–6pm; charge) was intended to form a monumental urban ensemble with the Hofburg opposite, though not all the planned buildings were completed. This huge neo-Renaissance palace houses five departments, all well worth spending time in. They include the **Egyptian and Near Eastern Collections**, **Greek and Roman Antiquities**, the **Coin Cabinet** and the **Kunstkammer** (Sculpture and Decorative Arts – under reconstruction for several years). However, by far the most popular section is the **Picture Gallery** **E**, one of the world's great collections of 16th- to 18th-century European art. Reflecting the acquisitive instincts of many a member of the Habsburg dynasty, its strengths lie in

Inside the Kunsthistorisches Museum

those areas which they once ruled or were closely associated with: the Netherlands, Spain, northern Italy and Germany. Thus the gallery has more than its fair share of the surviving paintings of Pieter Breughel the Elder (1526–69). These include three of his wonderful portrayals of the seasons, including the chilly *Hunters in the Snow*. Among other fine works from the Low Countries are paintings by Jan van Eyck, Rubens, Ruysdael, van Dyck and Vermeer, while Rembrandt is represented by a series of self-portraits. Italian works include canvases by Titian, Mantegna, Giorgioine and Caravaggio, as well as Raphael's much-loved *Madonna of the Meadows*. Dürer's *Martyrdom of the 10,000 Christians* is here, along with paintings by other German masters such as Cranach the Elder and Albrecht Altdorfer.

Though it attracts fewer visitors than its counterpart, the **Naturhistorisches Museum** (Natural History Museum; Thur–Mon 9am–6.30pm, Wed 9am–9pm; charge) is stuffed with treasures, many of them, like the specimens in the zoological section, literally so. The star exhibit, in the pre-history section, is the famous **Venus of Willendorf**, a busty little female statuette just 11cm (4ins) high and 25,000 years old.

The MuseumsQuartier

Vienna's **MuseumsQuartier** 🅕 is a large area where some of the city's best museums and galleries are concentrated. These are housed in a mixture of baroque and contemporary build-ings, which were renovated and built at huge expense, under-lining the Austrian capital's commitment to the arts.

The MuseumsQuartier

To the west of the two museums described above are the 18th-century Imperial Stables, converted in the first decade of the 21st cen-tury into a popular cultural complex. Restored to their original glory, the Baroque buildings are complemented by some sparkling new struc-tures, foremost among them one of the city's must-see art galleries; the **Leopold Museum** (daily 10am–6pm, Sept–May closed Tue; charge) houses an excep-tionally rich collection of 20th-century Austrian art, including the largest number of works by Schiele assem-bled anywhere. **MUMOK** (Museum of Modern Art;

Mon 2–7pm, Tue, Wed, Fri–Sun 10am–7pm, Thur until 9pm; charge) is devoted to international and contemporary art of the same era, though there are numerous Austrian works too. Temporary shows are held in the **Kunsthalle Wien** and exhibitions on architectural themes in the **Architektur Zentrum Wien**, while the **TanzQuartier** is a centre

Vienna City Hall

for contemporary dance. The **Zoom Kindermuseum** is an enthralling museum-cum-play-space for children.

Northern Ringstrasse

Beyond the Volksgarten, the Ring crosses the Rathausplatz, the setting for another group of pompous buildings. Completed in 1883, the neo-Gothic **Neues Rathaus** (New City Hall) was inspired by the great medieval town halls of Flanders, a style chosen to symbolise municipal power and glory.

Opposite the Rathaus, the **Burgtheater** of 1888 is one of the great stages of the German-speaking world. The grandiose neo-Renaissance building is flanked by substantial wings, whose sole function is to contain the two staircases, one for the public, the other for the Court.

The Rathausmann

On Emperor Franz Joseph's insistence, the tower of the City Hall was not allowed to overtop the 99m (325ft) spires of the nearby Votivkirche. The architect duly limited his tower to 98m (322ft), but slyly overcame the prohibition by topping it with the figure of the 3.4m (11ft) Rathausmann (a knight in armour).

The immensely long **Parlament** building was designed in the style of a Greek temple, a hopeful reference to the democratic traditions of Ancient Greece. It was completed in 1883 and provided in 1902 with a splendid fountain dominated by the figure of Pallas Athena, goddess of wisdom. The fact that she is looking *away* from the building – the scene of much folly in the past – has been the basis of many a Viennese witticism. The northern side of the Rathausplatz is overlooked by the University, which, as an institution, was founded in 1365, the second oldest in Central Europe.

Set back from the Ring to the north of the University, the neo-Gothic **Votivkirche** with its twin spires was begun in 1856 and only completed in 1879. It was intended as 'a monument of patriotism and devotion of the people to the Imperial House' following an assassination attempt on Franz Joseph in 1853.

Southern Ringstrasse

Located in the southern part of the city centre, the picture collection of the **Akademie der bildenden Künste** (Academy of Fine Arts; Tue–Sun 10am–6pm; charge) may not match that of the Kunsthistorisches Museum in quality and quantity, but it nevertheless has several first class Old Master paintings. Outstanding among them is Hieronymus Bosch's *Last Judgement*, with its terrifying depictions of the unspeakable tortures awaiting sinners. The Academy is notable for having refused to accept the young Adolf Hitler as a student, not once but twice. Its building, a typically ponderous neo-Renaissance Ringstrasse edifice, could not be more different in style from its neighbour, the **Secessionsgebäude** (Secession Building; Tue–Sun 10am–6pm; charge). Completed in 1898 by Jugendstil architect Joseph Maria Olbrich, this revolutionary structure was in effect the manifesto of the Vienna Secession movement of architects, designers and artists, as indicated by the motto above the entrance: *Der Zeit ihre Kunst, der Kunst ihre Freiheit* (To each Age its Art, to Art its Freedom). The interior has an extraordinary frieze painted by Gustav Klimt.

The key location of **Karlsplatz** in Vienna's public transport system is symbolised by the **Stadtbahn Pavillons**, two jewel-like little structures in steel, glass and marble designed in 1899 by city architect Otto Wagner as entrances to the city's Metropolitan Railway. The square, with its pond and Henry Moore sculpture, is the setting for a number of key buildings, none more dominant than the glorious **Karlskirche** **G** (Mon–Sat 9am–12.30pm, 1–6pm, Sun 1–6pm; charge). Commissioned in 1713 by Emperor Charles VI in thanks for deliverance from the plague, it is the masterpiece of the great Baroque architect Fischer von Erlach, though it had to be completed by his son after his death in 1723. It is a stunning and highly original synthesis of Roman columns, Greek portico and great dome, the interior of which is adorned with a fresco depicting the apotheosis of St Charles Borromeo, to whom the church is dedicated. Next to the church, the excellent **Wien Museum Karlsplatz** (Tue–Sun 9am–6pm; charge) is devoted to the history of Vienna. High points include fascinating models of the city

Detail of a Stadtbahn Pavillon at Karlsplatz

before and after the development of the Ringstrasse, and special displays on 'Vienna around 1900' dealing with the city at the zenith of its creativity. Opposite, the **Musikverein** is the home of the world-famous Vienna Philharmonic Orchestra.

The River Wien

Rising to the southwest in the Vienna Woods, the city's second river, with which it shares its name (the Wien), once flowed past the Karlskirche. By 1912 it had been put almost entirely underground, making space for the **Naschmarkt** to the southwest, the city's main produce market (and Saturday flea market). To make up for this treatment, the river was allowed to re-emerge further northeast along the Ring, where its banks were thoroughly beautified in Jugendstil style as part of the **Stadtpark** (City Park). The statuary here honours

Jugendstil

In Austria, Jugendstil (Art Nouveau) caught the imagination of the art world, and the result was the foundation of the Secession Movement by a group of renegade artists from the Academy in 1897. The central figure of the Secession was Gustav Klimt (1862–1918), whose erotic, fairytale-like painting style and themes came to embody Jugendstil. One of the key tenets for artists such as Klimt and Koloman Moser, and the leading Jugendstil architects Otto Wagner and Josef Hoffmann, was the linking of function and aesthetic.

Klimt's decorative elegance was a particular source of inspiration for Egon Schiele (1890–1918), whose linearity and subtlety reveal the strong influence of the Jugendstil. Schiele, however, emphasised expression over decoration, concentrating on the human figure with an acute eroticism that was less decorative than Klimt's. Evocation of intense feeling through colours and lines of equal importance to Oskar Kokoschka (1886–1980), a leading exponent of Expressionism.

many of the city's famous, none more so than **Johann Strauss the Younger**, with an iconic bronze and marble sculpture. At the far end of the park, the **MAK** (Applied Arts Museum; Tue 10am–10pm, Wed–Sun 10am–6pm; charge) is one of the finest of its kind in the world, excitingly redesigned in the 1990s by a bevy of contemporary artists. It cov-

Shopping at the Naschmarkt

ers its subject from Roman times onwards, with a natural emphasis on those periods when Austro-Hungarian designers were supreme, with wonderful displays of Bohemian glass, Biedermeier furniture and the classic products of the Wiener Werkstätte craft studios.

The Belvedere

One of the finest examples of Baroque large-scale architecture and landscape design, the **Belvedere** consists of two palaces, the **Oberes Belvedere** (Upper Belvedere) and the **Unteres Belvedere** (Lower Belvedere; both daily 10am–6pm; charge), linked by a sloping formal garden. The complex was built from 1714 onwards by Lukas von Hildebrandt for **Prince Eugene of Savoy** as his summer residence. The greatest and probably the wealthiest soldier ever to have served the Habsburgs, Eugene won the dynasty's eternal gratitude for pushing the Austrian frontier far into the Balkans in a series of spectacular victories over the Turks. Until his assassination in 1914, the palace served as Archduke Franz Ferdinand's Vienna base (he lived most of the time at Konopiště Castle in Bohemia).

Belvedere statuary

Relatively modest in scale, the Lower Belvedere was used as Eugene's private residence, but nevertheless has exceptionally sumptuous interiors, whose decor celebrates his military exploits. Together with the adjoining Orangery, it is used for temporary exhibitions. The Frenchman who designed the Belvedere gardens took advantage of the sloping site to create a wonderful composition of steps, ramps, formal planting and water bodies; from the terrace at the top there is an outstanding view of the city skyline. The monumental Upper Belvedere was less a residence than the place where Eugene entertained his guests. It is now the home of collections giving a comprehensive survey of Austrian art from medieval times onwards, though there are also contributions from other countries, including paintings by French Impressionists. But the greatest draw is Klimt's most celebrated work, *The Kiss*, as well as many lesser known works by Schiele and Kokoschka.

Beyond the Ringstrasse

Fans of the artist Friedensreich Hundertwasser (see page 64) head out to the Landstrasse District to his most admired building, the **Hundertwasserhaus** (not open to the public), a city housing scheme he redesigned, giving it his trademark irregular forms, undulating surfaces and bright colours.

Beyond the Belvedere, the **Heergeschichtliches Museum** (Military History Museum; daily 9am–5pm; charge) is of greater general interest than its name might suggest. There's plenty of weaponry and uniforms (some of the most gorgeous in the world), plus myriad works of art and other items exalting Imperial military exploits from the Thirty Years War onwards. The exhibit everyone comes to see, however, is the grand touring automobile in which Archduke Franz Ferdinand was assassinated, as well as his bloodstained tunic. Other items – including the surprise of a submarine – are reminders of Austria-Hungary's one-time status as a naval power.

Both ends of the Ringstrasse terminate at the winding Donaukanal (Danube Canal). Occupying a large part of the island between the Donaukanal and the much wider main channel, the **Prater** is Vienna's most extensive park, once reserved for the nobility but opened up to the public in 1766 by Emperor Joseph II.

Its most prominent feature is the funfair with the famous **Riesenrad** (Giant

Schloss Schönbrunn from the Privy Garden

Ferris Wheel), which was immortalised in the classic film noir *The Third Man*.

Schloss Schönbrunn

Like Louis XIV's Versailles, **Schloss Schönbrunn** ❶ (Apr–June, Sept–Oct daily 8.30am–5.30pm, July, Aug 8.30am–6.30pm, Nov–Mar 8.30am–5pm; charge) grew out of a late medieval hunting lodge, which was destroyed and rebuilt more than once by marauding Turks and Hungarians. After the Turkish siege was lifted in 1683, J.B. Fischer von Erlach was commissioned to build a palace which would have extended right up the hill to where the triumphal arch of the Gloriette now stands. Intended to outshine Versailles, this overambitious design was scaled down, and the palace eventually completed in the reign of Empress Maria Theresa has a mere 1,441 rooms.

Rich in historical associations, the palace is a treasure trove of 18th-century splendour, with paintings, tapestries, parquetry and panelling, mirrors and marble, lacquer panels, gilt and stucco used to show-stopping effect. A choice of tours introduces visitors to the key interiors. Some, like Maria Theresa's breakfast room, are quite intimate, others, like the Great Gallery, almost overwhelming in their pomp and circumstance. This is where the delegates to the 1815 Congress of Vienna forgot the affairs of state and danced the nights away, and where at a 1961 superpower summit, US President Kennedy encountered the Soviet leader Nikita Khruschev for the first time.

The palace's splendid park (Apr–Oct 6am–dusk, Nov–Mar from 6.30am) was open to the public in Imperial times, and is strolled in by millions every year. It's packed full of interest, with several follies, fountains and statuary, woodland, a zoo (Tiergarten), a set of botanical gardens, a huge tropical glasshouse (Palmenhaus), and a museum of coaches and carriages. But the dominating feature is the **Gloriette**, a vantage point with commanding views of the park and city.

Excursions from Vienna

On the west bank of the Danube just a few minutes away by suburban train, **Stift Klosterneuburg** (daily 9am–6pm) is one of Austria's most important monasteries. Visitors with their own transport can make the trip along the Höhenstrasse scenic road, taking in famous viewpoints at **Kahlenberg** and **Leopoldsberg**.

Cycling in Wienerwald
(Vienna Woods)

The monastery was founded in 1114 by Duke Leopold III, when the Babenbergs moved their court here from Melk. The Romanesque abbey church was given a thorough make over in the Baroque period, but the medieval cloisters are intact and the Leopoldkapelle has wonderful stained glass and a superb winged altarpiece. In complete contrast to the abbey and all it stands for is the **Sammlung Essl** (Essl Collection; Tue, Thur–Sun 10am–6pm, Wed 10am–9pm; charge). In a purpose-built, uncompromisingly modern structure, this is the largest private collection anywhere of post-war Austrian art, and probably the best place in which to get to grips with such movements as Abstract Expressionism and Vienna Actionism.

Wine villages

The city's *Heurige* (new season's wine) is best sampled in one of the taverns (confusingly named *Heuriger*) in the string of wine villages beautifully sited in the foothills of the Vienna Woods. The most popular and easily accessible is Grinzing, conveniently located at the terminus of the No.38 tram.

The Wienerwald

Anyone with a little time to spare should take advantage of Vienna's proximity to the glorious countryside of the **Wienerwald**, perhaps better translated as the Vienna Hills rather than the Vienna Woods. With vineyards and pretty villages and small towns as well as lovely woodlands, this area just beyond the southwestern edge of the city has traditionally been the place the Viennese enjoy bona fide countryside right on their doorstep. The rustic sights and sounds here inspired Beethoven's Sixth Symphony, the *Pastoral*.

The little town of **Percholdsdorf** is famous for its vineyards and its *Heuriger* taverns. Its inhabitants were able to save themselves on more than one occasion from the marauding Turks by locking themselves up in the Perchtoldsdorfer Turm. This massive medieval tower overlooks the marketplace, which is graced by a beautiful plague column. Further west, **Stift Heiligenkreuz** (Heiligenkreuz Abbey; charge) was founded, like Klosterneuburg, by Duke Leopold III in the early 13th century and endowed with a fragment of the Holy Cross. With a lovely church which has retained its

Burg Aggstein towering over the Danube

Romanesque facade, it is the oldest and largest Cistercian monastery in Europe.

From nearby Mayerling the road descends through the picturesque valley known as the Helenental, passing a brace of castle ruins before arriving at the spa town of **Baden**. The thermal waters here were known to the Romans, but Baden's glory days came in the early 19th century, when it enjoyed the patronage of court and gentry; with its Biedermeier villas and Kurpark, it still exudes the faded charm of those days. The vineyards laid out on southeast-facing slopes of the Wienerwald produce famous vintages, best tasted in attractive places like **Gumpoldskirchen** and **Mödling**.

LOWER AUSTRIA

The province of Lower Austria (Niederösterreich) completely surrounds Vienna, though since 1987 the provincial capital has not been here but in the much smaller town of St Pölten. The province's main artery is the mighty Danube, with much to interest the visitor both upstream and downstream from Vienna. The most picturesque stretch of the river passes through the Wachau district, which is one of the country's most visited regions, its highlight the great Baroque abbey at Melk. The more out-of-the-way Weinviertel and Waldviertel districts have a lower profile, but contain many hidden treasures and are well worth exploring.

Downstream from Vienna

Leaving Vienna, the Danube flows east towards its confluence with the River March and the Slovak capital Bratislava, a mere 65km (40 miles) away. To the north of the river is the **Marchfeld**, a monotonous flat borderland crossed and recrossed by many an army on its way to or from Vienna and the scene of a many a decisive battle in Austrian and European history. With its easy access to Vienna, the Marchfeld was also a favoured residential and sporting location for royalty and aristocracy, and is studded with numerous castles and country houses. Once freed from the confines of the city, the Danube takes on a surprisingly natural character. As well as the main waterway, there are oxbow lakes, quiet side channels, water meadows, riverine woods of poplar and willow, and an intriguing display of wildlife.

The whole area is designated a national park; a good place to begin an exploration of its unusual landscapes is in the village of Orth, where **Schloss Orth** (late Mar–Sept 9am–6pm, Oct–Nov 9am–5pm; charge) houses a national park centre, a viewing tower and a museum. Storks appreciate this watery borderland, and in summer dozens of breeding pairs can be observed at a World Wildlife sanctuary at **Marchegg** right on the border with Slovakia. Of the Marchfeld castles, lavishly restored **Schlosshof** (Apr–Oct

10am–6pm; charge) is the most intriguing. Built in 1725 for the illustrious Prince Eugene of Savoy by the great Baroque architect Hildebrandt, it has sumptuous interiors, terraced gardens, a magnificent orangery and outbuildings which include a working distillery.

On the south bank of the Danube, a short drive from Schlosshof, is the old frontier fortress town of **Hainburg**, still with some of its ramparts including a trio of gateways, of which the massive 13th-century Wiener Tor is the most striking. To the west of Hainburg, and, in its time, far more important, is **Carnuntum** (mid-Mar–mid-Nov Mon 9am–5pm; charge), founded by Emperor Tiberius in 6AD and at its fullest extent home to tens of thousands of Roman citizens and to soldiers guarding the Danube frontier. Stretching for several kilometres between Bad Deutsch-Altenburg and Petronell, this one-time capital of the province of Upper Pannonia is

Roman remains at Carnuntum

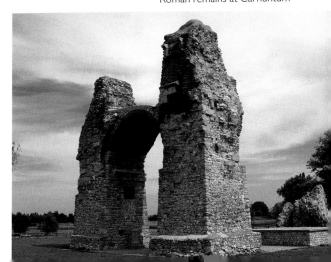

The square in Retz

one of the largest and most important Roman sites in Central Europe, with plenty to see, including original and meticulously reconstructed public baths, gardens and amphitheatres as well as a well-stocked museum.

Music-lovers will want to make the short pilgrimage southwards to the village of **Rohrau** to pay homage to one of Austria's best-loved composers at his birthplace: as well as the **Geburtshaus Joseph Haydn** (Tue–Sun 10am–4pm; charge), a charming thatched building with an arcaded courtyard, Rohrau also has a **Schloss** (Easter–Oct Tue–Sun 10am–5pm; charge), which houses the aristocratic Harrach family's Old Masters, one of the largest private collections of its kind.

Upstream from Vienna

True to its name, Lower Austria's fertile and sunny **Weinviertel** (Wine District) is the country's main wine-producing region. Agriculture flourishes too, while to the east of the main road to the Czech border there is an important oil and gas field. More interesting than the rather dull landscape are the wine villages and small towns with their characteristic vintners' houses and rows of wine cellars laid out along sunken lanes. All kinds of traditional buildings from the region can be seen at the **Weinviertler Museumsdorf** (Open-Air Museum; mid-Apr–Oct 9.30am–6pm; charge) at Niedersulz, where they have been cleverly grouped together to give the impression of a real village rather than just a collection of individual structures. Among the main wine towns are **Poysdorf** and **Asparn an der Zaya**, while **Laa an der Thaya** is more famous for its beer, with a brewing museum in its Schloss. But the star among the Weinviertel's towns is **Retz ❷**, with a procession of historic buildings gracing its splendidly spacious square. Beneath the streets, and covering a more extensive area, is a 20km (12-mile) network of wine cellars up to 30m (100ft) deep, parts of which can be explored in the course of a guided tour (May–Oct daily 10.30am, 2pm, 4pm, Nov–Dec, Mar–Apr 2pm, Jan–Feb Sat–Sun 2pm; charge).

The **Waldviertel** (Forest District) also lives up to its name, with more than a third of its area carpeted in woodland. Although somewhat off the beaten track, it nevertheless attracts visitors in search of peace and quiet, and has become more popular since the fall of the Iron Curtain and the opening up of the border with the Czech Republic. Czech and Austrian cooperation is evident in the designation of the lovely winding gorge of the River Thaya as the **Nationalpark Thayatal/ Národní park Podyjí**, a cross-border national park. There's a park information centre at delightful little **Hardegg**, the smallest town in Austria, dominated from a crag by its stern medieval **Burg** (daily July–Aug

Hardegg Castle

9am–6pm, Apr–June, Sept–Nov 9am–5pm; charge), the origins of which go back to the 10th century.

In complete contrast, though in the same ownership and a few kilometres to the west, is elegant **Schloss Riegersburg** (daily Apr–June, Sept–Oct 9am–5pm, July, Aug 9am–7pm; charge), a splendidly furnished Baroque palace set among lakes and with an unusual feature, a dog cemetery. Between the Thaya valley and the Danube, other highlights of the region command attention. As well as a fine square with a plague column, the old town of **Eggenburg** boasts the **Österreichisches Motorradmuseum** (Austrian Motorcycle Museum; mid-Mar–mid-Nov Sat, Sun 10am–5pm; charge) with a fabulous collection of two-wheelers of all kinds. Enthroned among the woods above the winding River Kamp is **Stift Altenburg** (daily Easter–Oct; charge), one of the country's

Durnstein, overlooked by its famous castle

finest abbey complexes, comparable with the more accessible and far more visited Stift Melk.

The Wachau and Stift Melk

For nearly 40km (25 miles), the broad Danube cuts its winding way through a granite plateau, passing crag-top castle ruins, famous vineyards, and apricot orchards

A friendly encounter

which burst into blossom come springtime. Known as the **Wachau** ❸, and protected from unsuitable development by Unesco World Heritage designation, this almost excessively picturesque stretch of the river is one of the country's most popular tourist destinations, the classic mode of travel being a trip aboard a steamer belonging to the famous Danube Steam Navigation Company. The eastern approach to the Wachau is guarded by the old wine-growing town of **Krems**, which merges westwards with its neighbours, the oddly named **Und** (meaning 'and') and **Stein**. Climbing up the hillside and with a wealth of old buildings testifying to its medieval and later prosperity, Krems is a delight to wander.

A good account of local history, with a natural emphasis on the role of viticulture, is provided by the town's **Weinstadt Museum** (Wed–Sat 10am–6pm, Sun 1–6pm; charge), housed in a former monastery. A 15-minute walk to the west via the two gateways of Steiner Tor and Kremser Tor, Stein is smaller and quieter than Krems and even better preserved. Visible from the upper parts of both towns, some distance away on the far side of the Danube, the hilltop monastery of **Stift Göttweig** (daily late Mar–mid-Nov; charge) was founded in

The baroque Stift Melk

the 11th century but was rebuilt in the early 18th century by Johann Lukas von Hildebrandt. His greatest achievement here is the masterly Imperial Staircase, its pomp further enhanced by a ceiling fresco by Paul Troger.

Just northeast of Krems, the historic and extremely picturesque little town of **Langenlois** may be small but nevertheless claims to be Austria's largest wine town. History and modernity are combined in its **Loisium** (Apr–Oct daily 10am–7pm, Nov–Mar Tue–Sun 10am–7pm; charge), where a stunningly contemporary metallic cube of a visitor centre and 1.5km (1 mile) of ancient wine cellars tell the story of wine making in an excitingly innovative way.

The first place of note upstream from Krems is the tiny walled town of **Dürnstein** with its landmark blue and white church tower. High above is the ruined castle where the imprisoned King Richard the Lionheart of England was discovered by his faithful minstrel Blondel.

Other exquisite little towns follow, including **Burg Aggstein**, an awesome castle ruin perched some 300m (1000ft) above the river and built by a dynasty of robber barons who grew rich by plundering passing vessels. But the most imposing landmark in the area is without doubt **Stift Melk ❹** (daily May–Sept 9am–5.30pm, Apr, Oct 9am–4.30pm; charge), the great Baroque monastery stretching the length of a granite promontory and almost dwarfing the urban settlement at its foot. This strategic site has been called the 'cradle of Austria', since it was from here in the early Middle Ages that the Babenberger dukes ruled the 'Ostmark', the frontier region at the eastern extremity of the Holy Roman Empire. When they moved their seat to Vienna in 1089, they granted Melk to the Benedictines who have been here ever since. During the Turkish troubles at the end of the 17th century the monastery burnt down, and was rebuilt at the start of the 18th century on a truly palatial scale. From its terrace overlooking town and river, to its church, marble hall and 100,000-volume library, Melk is a triumph of Baroque architecture and interior design, the work of some of the greatest names of the time including

Richard Lionheart

King Richard had refused to share the booty accumulated during the Third Crusade of 1191 with Austrian Duke Leopold V. Making his way back from the Holy Land in disguise, Richard was recognised in Vienna, arrested, and imprisoned at Dürnstein. The legend has it that Blondel tracked his master down when Richard took up the refrain the minstrel had sung outside his dungeon. The king nevertheless had to languish in jail a further twelve months before a huge ransom could be raised and delivered to Leopold, who spent it on building Vienna's first city wall.

the architect Jakob Prandtauer and the fresco painter Paul Troger. Attracting hundreds of thousands of visitors every year, it was also the inspiration for Umberto Eco's novel *The Name of the Rose*.

Upstream from Melk, a short distance inland from the north bank of the Danube, seven-towered **Schloss Artstetten** (Apr–Oct daily 9am–5.30pm; charge) was one of the residences of Archduke Franz Ferdinand (1863–1914), the Habsburg heir to the throne whose assassination at Sarajevo in June 1914 lit the blue touchpaper of World War I. An extensive exhibition entitled 'For Heart and Crown' celebrates the life and chronicles the precipitate end of the unfortunate Archduke (see page 23).

BURGENLAND

A sliver of land running parallel to the border with Hungary, little Burgenland is the easternmost and least 'Austrian' of the country's provinces. A region of low hills merging with the steppe-like landscapes of the Hungarian *puszta* (plain), it only became part of Austria after World War I, hav-

Cherry trees in Burgenland

ing previously been ruled from Budapest. However, its natural capital, the old city of Ödenburg, remained with Hungary (as Sopron), and the town and the area immediately around it still protrude into Austrian territory, almost dividing Burgenland in two. The Burgenland's hill country is attractive enough, but the province's two great attractions are its miniature capital, Eisenstadt, and its great lake, the Neusiedler See.

Eisenstadt

With a population of just 12,000, this pretty little town owes its fame to the princely **Esterházy** family, stout defenders of the Empire against the Turks and great patrons of the arts, notably in their employment of the composer **Josef Haydn** (1732–1809) who was born at nearby Rohrau and remained in the family's service for 30 years. The Esterházys still own Eisenstadt's magnificent Baroque **Schloss Esterházy**

Lighthouse on Lake Neusiedl

(Apr–mid-Nov 9am–6pm daily, mid-Nov–Mar 9am–5pm weekends; charge); of the palace's 200-plus rooms, the grandest is the acoustically perfect Haydnsaal, where the composer conducted many a performance. His home, the **Haydnhaus** (daily Apr–Oct 9am–5pm; charge) can be inspected, while his mausoleum is in the **Bergkirche** (daily Apr–Oct; charge), a Baroque church built on rising ground in the western part of town. The church also has an extraordinary **Kalvarienberg** (Calvary), whose labyrinthine Stations of the Cross feature 200 life-size figures in dramatic poses.

The later Esterházys preferred the comforts of their town palace to those of their fortress, **Burg Forchenstein** (Apr–Oct daily 10am–6pm; charge). Built on a commanding site overlooking the Hungarian plain 20km (12 miles) southwest of Eisenstadt, this great stronghold never fell to the Turks, and its arsenal contains many trophies captured from them as well as masses of weaponry used by the Esterházy regiments.

Neusiedler See

Shared with Hungary, though mostly in Austria, this vast (320 sq km/125 sq mile) and shallow lake fulfils a dual role as an extremely popular recreation area and a nature reserve of international significance. Fed only by precipitation and with no outflow, the lake has a maximum depth of 2m (6ft). Vineyards surround the lake, which in many places is separated from the shoreline by extensive reed beds. Together with the marshlands of the **Seewinkl** in its southeastern corner, these are a vital habitat, a home for some 300 bird species, including many rare types. The best place to find out about the area's wildlife is to visit the **Nationalpark Informationszentrum** (Apr–Oct Mon–Fri 8am–5pm, Sat–Sun 10am–5pm, Nov–Mar daily 8am–4pm) just outside the village of Illmitz. Elsewhere, water sports are the activity many come to enjoy; the region's hot summers warm the lake quickly, making swimming very agreeable, while yachtspeople and windsurfers can usually rely on a breeze.

The most attractive places around the lake are **Rust**, as well-known for its wines as for the storks that nest on its chimney tops, and **Mörbisch**, with a main street of spotless whitewashed dwellings garnished with flowers and dried corn cobs.

STYRIA

Calling itself Austria's 'Green Heart', the country's southeastern province stretches from the Alps to the hills and plains bordering Slovenia and Hungary. Less well-known to visitors from abroad than some of the other provinces, it offers a huge

Delightful Mariazell

variety of scenery and a number of unique attractions, not least its characterful capital, **Graz ⑤**.

Graz

Overlooked by the rocky height of the **Schlossberg**, Graz commands the crossing over the swiftly flowing River Mur as it emerges from the Alpine foothills into a broad and fertile basin. This has always been a strategically important site, inhabited in pre-Roman times as well as by 6th-century Slavs, who gave it the name *gradec*, meaning fortified place. In 1379 it became the residence of a branch of the ruling Habsburg dynasty, a prestigious position it maintained for more than two centuries. Then, for an equal length of time, it served as a bulwark against the Turkish advance into central Europe. Lacking the Alpine setting that lends other provincial capitals their special glamour, but sometimes threatens to overwhelm them with sheer numbers of visitors, Graz is nevertheless a fascinating city, full of historic interest, with an exceptionally lively cultural scene and a youthful attitude to life, thanks not least to its high student population.

Life in Graz revolves around the bustling **Hauptplatz**, the triangular central square and main tram stop, and, running off it, pedestrianised **Herrengasse**, the city's central thoroughfare. 17th- and 18th-century facades line two sides of the square, at the centre of which rises a statue of the Styrians' favourite Habsburg, Archduke Johann, flanked by female figures symbolising the historic province's four rivers. Forming the third side of the square and turning the corner with Herrengassse is the **Rathaus**, a pompous 19th-century building in neo-Renaissance style. In Herrengasse itself, the mid-16th-century **Landhaus** is a genuine Renaissance palace, one of the finest of its kind north of the Alps. The stately edifice with its superb three-storey arcaded courtyard was built by the Italian master architect Domenico dell'Allio to house the Styrian Diet, and is still the home of the province's parliament. Next door, the 17th-century **Zeughaus** (Arsenal; Apr–Oct Wed–Mon 10am–5pm; charge) was the largest in the world when it was built in the mid-17th century. It is still unique in its state of perfect preservation, with a vast array of muskets, pistols, swords, crossbows, cannon, and armour for men and horses, more than enough to equip an army of tens of thousands.

Between Herrengasse and the government offices in the 15th-century **Burg** (Castle) to the northeast is the most fascinating part of old Graz. Narrow **Sporgasse** has a number of fine old buildings, while the restaurant and bar area around Mehlplatz and Färberplatz, nicknamed the 'Bermuda Triangle', buzzes with life from the early evening onwards. In aptly named Glockenspielplatz, a pair of wooden figures in traditional costume emerge three times daily (at 11am, 3pm and 6pm) to entertain the crowds. The late 15th-century Gothic **Domkirche** (Cathedral) has a remarkable external

View over Graz

wall-painting showing the city threatened by plague, locusts and Turks. Next door, the splendid domed **Mausoleum** was begun in 1614 by Emperor Ferdinand II as his last resting place, though he is buried elsewhere.

The Schlossberg

This 472m (1,548ft) high block of dolomite overlooking the city formed a perfect site for a citadel and remains one of its great assets today, having been transformed into parkland after the fortifications were razed during the French siege in 1809. The hill can be climbed on foot from the Stadtpark, by zigzagging stairs or lift from Sackstrasse, or by a century-old funicular, which deposits passengers close to the **Glockenturm**, a tower with a monster bell which is rung three times daily. Lower down, the distinctive 13th-century **Uhrturm** (Clock Tower) is a city emblem. There are wonderful views over the red rooftops, as well as of the west bank of the Mur, where the lovely twin-towered Baroque **Mariahilf-Kirche** is comprehensively upstaged by the city's art gallery, the **Kunsthaus Graz** (Tue–Sun 10am–5pm; charge). Completed in 2003, and referred to as the 'friendly alien' by local people, this bulbous blue glass structure with its odd protrusions is a venue for changing exhibitions of contemporary art. It has a compatible companion in the upstream **Murinsel**. This curving, zoomorphic structure spanning the river houses a café and a little amphitheatre, and was an integral part of Graz's time in the sun as European City of Culture in 2003.

Schloss Eggenberg
In its landscaped park at the foot of the green hills on the western edge of the city stands **Schloss Eggenberg** (Apr–Oct

Friedensreich Hundertwasser

Born plain Friedrich Stowasser in Vienna in 1928, this *enfant terrible* of the art world had such strongly held views about world peace, environmental destruction, man, art and nature that he changed his name to Friedensreich Regentag Dunkelbunt Hundertwasser (Peace-rich, Rainday, Darkly Colourful, Hundredwater – 'sto' means 'hundred' in the languages of neighbouring Slavic countries). Starting as a painter inspired by the likes of Klimt and Schiele, he soon turned to architecture and landscape, taking as his model the Catalan architect Antoni Gaudí.

His habit of giving lectures in the nude and his promotion of his bedside, waterless toilet brought him much attention, and eventually architectural commissions, three of which are in Styria, though his best-known work is the Hundertwasser Haus in Vienna. His wobbly-looking, colourful buildings bear out typical Hundertwasser aphorisms such as 'The straight line is godless' and 'Life is poorer without kitsch'. He died in 2000 aboard the QE2 liner while returning from New Zealand, his adoptive home.

Tue–Sun 10am–4pm; charge), the palace built by Hans Ulrich von Eggenberg in 1625 and which was declared a Unesco World Cultural Heritage Site in 2010. As well as expressing the prestige won by Eggenberg in the course of a meteoric career in the service of Emperor Ferdinand II, the building is designed as an allegory of cosmic harmony. Four towers represent the points of the compass, 12 gates the months of the year, 24 state rooms the hours of

Making glass

the day, and so on. The festival hall known as the Planetensaal is particularly richly decorated. A newly laid-out garden, the Planetengarten, complements the symbolism of the palace.

Excursions from Graz

One of Austria's most fascinating open-air museums is located in a secluded wooded valley on the banks of the Mur some 18km (11 miles) north of Graz. The **Österreichisches Freilichtmuseum** (Apr–Oct daily 9am–5pm; charge) at **Stübing** has examples of traditional buildings from all over Austria, from the thatched cottages of Burgenland and the stone-built structures of the Danube lands to the timber chalets of the Alps, all laid out in geographical order from east to west. As well as houses and farmsteads, there are watermills and smithies, even a fire station and a well-stocked village shop.

To the northwest, not far from the industrial town of Köflach, the **Lipizzaner Welt Piber** (Lipizzaner Stud; Apr–Oct Tue–Sun 9am–5.30pm; charge) is the home

Vineyard in the south of Styria

ground of the snow-white stallions supplied to Vienna's Riding School. The extensive estate, laid out at the foot of a lovely Baroque schloss, has stables, an arena, a museum and a blacksmith's, and offers the chance of getting up close to the famous beasts themselves. As well as a flourishing glass-making tradition, the nearby village of **Bärnbach** boasts a post-war church that was given a thorough makeover in 1987 by Friedensreich Hundertwasser. The idiosyncratic artist transformed the otherwise plain building by eliminating as many straight lines as possible, introducing colour and irregular forms and filling the churchyard with gateways representing the world's religions.

Styrian vineyards and spas

Around 7 percent of Austria's wine is produced in Styria, and the province is blessed with some of the country's most picturesque vineyards, none prettier than those along the border with Slovenia some 40km (25 miles) south of Graz. With its farmhouses scattered among the friendly, sun-drenched little hills, and with poplar trees standing in for cypresses, the area is deservedly called 'Styrian Tuscany'. A unique feature is the *Klapotetz*, a windmill-like structure which in fact is a giant rattle designed to scare away birds. The region is geared up for wine tourism, with plenty of rustic places to stay, wine tasting at a *Buschenschank* (the local equivalent of a Vienna *Heuriger*), the dispensing of *Sturm*, a lightly fermented grape juice, and the autumn consumption of roast chestnuts. There are wine festivals in places like the large village of **Gamlitz**, which also has a wine museum. Nearby **Ehrenhausen** on the River Mur has a most attractive square, overlooked from its hilltop site by the elaborate mausoleum of the Eggenberg family.

Long-extinct volcanoes helped form the fertile landscape of southeastern Styria, which is renowned for its spa resorts, its crag-top castles, and for the savoury oil from its abundant harvest of pumpkins. Separated from Slovenia only by the Mur, **Bad Radkersburg** is an ancient stronghold and trading place, with a fine main square, the remains of fortifications and a modern spa quarter. To the north, **Bad Gleichenberg** has a longer pedigree as a place to take the waters, having been known to the Romans. Its great days came however in the 19th century, when elegant villas were built and a leafy Kurpark laid out. Nearby is **Styrassic Park** (Mar–Oct daily 9am–5pm; charge), a theme park where dozens of life-size models

Styrassic Park

Lake Erlauf

of prehistoric monsters lurk menacingly among the trees. Perched 482m (1,581ft) up on what is left of the core of an old volcano, the castle of **Riegersburg** ❻ (daily May–Sept 9am–5pm, Apr, Oct 10am–5pm; charge) is an astonishing sight. Its location alone would seem enough to deter would-be attackers, though a succession of owners strengthened it with gateways, bastions, and miles of walls. Once a major deterrent to the Ottoman advance, the great fortress today houses interestingly conceived displays on historical themes such as religious intolerance and the persecution of witches. To the northeast, the fortunes of **Bad Blumau** were revived when Friedensreich Hundertwasser designed the Rogner Spa, letting his imagination run free with colourful, strangely shaped buildings which nevertheless seem in complete harmony with the surrounding landscape.

Mariazell

The valley of the River Mur leads northwards from Graz to busy **Bruck an der Mur**, an important road and rail junction and industrial town. The ironworking traditions of the region are evident in the handsome main square, its focal point a wonderful wrought-iron fountain dating from 1626. Further north still, among the forests on the mountainous border with Lower Austria, is **Mariazell** ❼, Austria's most important place of pilgrimage. The tiny town of some 2,000 souls welcomes around 1 million pilgrims every year, drawn here from all over Central Europe and the Balkans by a miracle-working statue of the Virgin Mary. Dating from the 12th century, the little wooden figure was credited with the victory of King Louis of Hungary over the Turks in 1377, and when the Habsburgs later placed their realm under her protection, her popularity was assured. The medieval basilica in which she is housed was rebuilt and extended in the 17th century to cater for the growing number of pilgrims, though the architect retained the original Gothic spire between his typically Baroque twin towers. After completing their devotions, pilgrims can take a summertime steam tram to nearby **Lake Erlauf** or a cable car up the **Bürgeralpe**, the local mountain.

Leoben

Back in the valley of the Mur, Styria's second-largest town, historic **Leoben**, has an ironworking tradition going back to the Middle Ages. The ore processed here was brought down from **Vordernberg** and especially from **Eisenerz**. Literally meaning 'Iron Ore', the town of Eisenerz is dominated by the monstrous ziggurat of the Erzberg, the 'Iron Mountain' which rises more than 700m (2,300ft) above the valley floor in a series of terraces formed by opencast mining. The town itself has many fascinating relics of past mining days, including a fortified church, a bell tower which rang out the miners' changes of shift, and an excellent **Stadtmuseum** (Apr–Oct Tue–Sun 10am–4pm; charge). The museum is housed in the Kammerhof, originally the seat of the imperial mining administration, and subsequently a hunting lodge for Emperor Franz Josef. But the most popular attraction in town is a visit to the underground mine,

Hiking in Ramsau

the **Schaubergwerk**, which is combined with a ride around the mountain aboard 'Hauly', a gargantuan ore transporter (May–Oct daily 10am–3pm; charge).

At the old iron-working settlement of Hieflau, the River Enns emerges from the 15km (9-mile) **Gesäuse gorge** ❽, one of the wildest and most spectacular landscapes in Austria. Designated a national park in 2002, the 1,700m (5,580ft) deep gorge was cut by the raging waters of the Enns through the limestone massif of the Ennstaler Alps, whose shining, jagged peaks rise dramatically over dark coniferous forests. The area is a climbers' paradise, and there is exciting rafting on the river's foaming waters. Beyond the western entrance to the gorge stands **Stift Admont**, a Benedictine abbey founded in the 11th century by St Emma from Carinthia. The abbey had to be rebuilt after a fire in 1865, but its great treasure, the **Library** (Apr–Oct daily 10am–5pm; charge) was spared; a jewel of Rococo art and architecture, it has more than 200,000 books and manuscripts, glorious ceiling frescoes and an awe-some quartet of carved figures representing Death, Heaven, Hell and the Last Judgement.

Dachstein

The upper valley of the Enns is overlooked from the north by the sheer walls and crags of the limestone **Dachstein ❾** massif, and from the south by the gentler summits of the Niedere Tauern range. Here are Styria's most dramatic Alpine landscapes, popular in both summer and winter, with endless possibilities for hiking and skiing. At the centre of the region stands the town of **Schladming**, whose late medieval prosperity depended on the silver, copper, nickel and lead extracted from the mountains. In 1525 Protestant miners joined forces with the local peasantry in a great rebellion, which was savagely put down; Schladming was burnt to the ground in reprisal, and only regained its town status four centuries later, in 1925. Nowadays it is famous for hosting prestigious downhill skiing events. Among the meadows on the sunny, south-facing plateau high above, the scattered settlement of **Ramsau** enjoys equal fame as a centre for cross-country skiing, with a 150km (90-mile) network of *loipen* (trails).

Stift Admont

A toll road winds up to the lower station of the Dachstein cable car, which takes just a few minutes to hoist its passengers past the terrifying, near-vertical south face of the Dachstein to the 2,700m (8,856ft) **Hunerkogel ❿**. From this privileged viewpoint there are extraordinary views down on the glacier,

as well as an all-round panorama of much of the Austrian Alps. Additional attractions include the exposed 'Skywalk' around the top station and the 'Dachstein Ice Palace', a grotto hollowed out into the glacier, which has been decorated with eerily lit icy sculptures.

CARINTHIA AND EAST TYROL

Austria's southernmost province stretches from the glaciers of the Hohe Tauern national park in the central Alps to the jagged limestone peaks forming the border with Italy and Slovenia. In between are lower mountains and lovely valleys, some of them filled with shining lakes. With hard winters and hot summers guaranteeing year-round outdoor fun, Carinthia justifiably styles itself the country's holiday paradise, not least because, unlike in most Alpine countries, the lake waters become invitingly warm from late springtime onwards. This has contributed to a sophisticated, almost Riviera-like holiday ambience along the shore of the largest lake, Wörthersee.

Klagenfurt city centre

Klagenfurt

What is now Carinthia's capital city was established in the middle of the 13th century close to the eastern shore of Lake Wörthersee in order to act as a rival to Villach, a far more ancient foundation. A series of great fires and subsequent rebuilds means that little remains of the original town, which was greatly extended in the early 16th century along carefully planned lines, with a chequerboard layout of streets and squares and a rectangle of fortifications which have long since given way to the ring road. Subsequent prosperity led to the construction of many fine buildings, notably to the dozens of palaces and town mansions with arcaded courtyards which contribute much to the city's charm and its Italianate atmosphere. Perhaps less obviously glamorous than other Austrian provincial capitals, Klagenfurt is full of interest, and makes a good urban base for exploring this part of Carinthia.

The classic starting point for an urban exploration is the spacious **Neuer Platz**, the 'New Square', which formed the focal point of the replanned 16th-century town. The dominant building is the Rathaus, a stately Renaissance palace, which has served as the town hall since 1918. However, what really catches the eye is the central fountain with its famous sculpture of the dragon-like Lindwurm, the city's emblem. To the north of Neuer Platz is the original core of the city, a web of traffic-free streets and lanes centred on

The Klagenfurt Lindwurm

Legend has it that this winged and curly tailed beast once terrorised traders making their way through the marshlands on which Klagenfurt was subsequently built. It was eventually confronted by a pair of bold swordsmen, who concealed themselves in a tower, then sallied forth to slay the terrible monster as it feasted on a tethered cow. The sculptor who created the Lindwurm statue in 1593 used a fragment of real monster as his model, the skull of a prehistoric rhinoceros. Spouting water from its open jaw, the *Wurm* is guarded by a Hercules figure brandishing a club.

Alter Platz (Old Square), where it is a pleasure to wander, window-shop and peek in to at least some of the numerous charming courtyards. In summer there are plenty of open-air cafés and restaurants in which to take your ease and soak up the almost Mediterranean ambience. On the west side of Alter Platz is the city's oldest building, the 15th-century Haus zur Goldenen Gans (Golden Goose Building) with earthquake-resistant buttresses. Further west, along Herrengasse, is the Renaissance **Landhaus**, the seat of the provincial government, whose spectacular **Wappensaal** (Heraldic Hall; Apr–Oct Mon–Sat 9am–5pm; charge) features no fewer than 665 colourful coats of arms. Nearby is the **Hauptpfarrkirche St Egid** (City Church) with a tower (Mon–Fri 10am–5.30pm, Sat 10am–12.30pm; charge) that can be climbed for an overall view of the town in its setting. Keen museum-goers wanting to find out more about the history, geology and folk culture of Carinthia should head for the **Landesmuseum** (Provincial Museum; Tue–Fri 10am–6pm, Sat–Sun 10am–5pm; charge) in the southern part of the city centre, where one of the star exhibits is a huge relief model of the Grossglockner massif.

The spectacular Wappensaal, Landhaus

In summertime, city-dwellers flock westward to the shores of Wörthersee, some of them aboard the pleasure boat that sails along the **Lendkanal**, the old waterway dug to connect Klagenfurt with the lake. Here, as well as steamer landing stages and an extensive lido there is the immensely popular **Minimundus** (Mar, Apr, Oct

Portschach am Wörthersee

9am–6pm, May–June, Sept 9am–7pm, July–Aug 9am–8pm;
charge). As its name implies, this is a world in miniature, with
more than 150 scale models of famous buildings from around
the globe, all in an attractive garden setting.

Wörthersee

The largest and possibly the loveliest of Carinthia's lakes,
the curvaceous **Wörthersee** ⓫ stretches for some 16km
(10 miles) westward from Klagenfurt's lakeshore to the
resort of Velden. Enclosed by gloriously wooded hills and
with ever-changing views of the high mountains beyond,
it reaches a depth of 85m (275ft), despite which its waters
warm rapidly in early summer to make bathing a pleasur-
able experience. Yachts, water-skiers and windsurfers share
its surface with the fleet of white pleasure steamers, a trip
aboard one of which is the best introduction to the lake
and its setting.

Maria Wörth

Wörthersee's great popularity began when the railway from Vienna to the Adriatic was built along its northern shore in 1863; almost immediately, prosperous Viennese started to holiday here, and part of the lake's attractiveness is due to the architecturally extravagant Victorian villas and turn-of-the-century hotels built to accommodate them. The sunny north shore is more developed than the slightly shadier south, which remains relatively tranquil.

Vying for first place among the fashion-conscious are the busy resorts of **Pörtschach** and **Velden**, both with lakeside promenades, an array of places to stay and eat, and a general atmosphere of Riviera-style hedonism. Pörtschach has a park-like peninsula protruding into the lake, while Velden is laid out in a gracious curve around its western extremity. As well as a modern casino, Velden also has the **Schloss**, built originally as a baronial hunting lodge in the 16th century, burnt down, then rebuilt as a luxury hotel in the 1920s. In the 1990s it became famous all over the German-speaking world as an ever-present background in a TV soap opera *Ein Schloss am Wörthersee*. In the mid-noughties it was lavishly upgraded and is now a five-star establishment.

The villages along the south shore of the lake do not attempt to match Velden and Pörtschach for sophistication, but have plenty of allure of their own. In the past they have attracted residents such as Gustav Mahler, who found the area congenial for his compositions, as well as the Vienna Boys' Choir who spent holidays together here. Opposite Pörtschach is the tiny settlement of **Maria Wörth** ⓑ, which, with its two churches picturesquely perched on the rocky outcrops of its peninsula, has become the symbol of the Wörthersee. The older and larger of the two churches dates originally from the 9th century when it was founded by German missionaries bent on converting the heathen Slavs who then dominated the region. It has preserved its Romanesque crypt as well as a wealth of interior furnishings. Topping the heights to the south of Maria Wörth is the **Pyramidenkogel** (Apr–Oct daily; charge), a 54m (177ft) viewing tower offering a fabulous panorama over half of Carinthia.

North of Klagenfurt

Known as the Zollfeld, the plain stretching north from Klagenfurt has always been the heartland of Carinthia. Virunum, the now-vanished Romano-Celtic capital of the province of Noricum was located here, its stones later plundered to help build the hilltop Christian pilgrimage site of **Maria Saal**. Opposite the arcaded charnel house, the pilgrimage church's porch incorporates a Roman gravestone depicting the she-wolf suckling Romulus and Remus. Further northeast, at the extensive **Archäologischer Park Magdalensberg** (May–Oct daily 9am–6pm; charge), the Roman city built over an earlier Celtic settlement has been excavated and partly restored. Here too there is a pilgrimage church atop a mountain, with fine vistas of the surrounding area. But by far the most spectacular hilltop feature of the region is **Burg Hochosterwitz** ⓭ (daily May–Sept 9am–6pm, Apr, Oct 9am–5pm; charge), a stunning fortress which is said to have given Walt Disney his idea of how a medieval stronghold should look. A lift crawls up the face of the 150m (500ft) limestone crag on which the castle is built, but it's more rewarding to walk up and pass through the 14 fortified gateways which helped make Hochosterwitz utterly impregnable. The castle's present appearance dates from the late 16th century, when it was rebuilt on the orders of Carinthia's governor, Georg von Khevenhüller, primarily to guard his realm from the Turkish peril.

The principal urban centre of the Zollfeld is **St Veit an der Glan**, a fine old town whose elongated main square is lined with colourful buildings of various ages. Prominent among them is the Rathaus, with a Baroque facade and a lovely Renaissance courtyard with a modern glazed roof. But perhaps the most fascinating building in town is the fantastical red, white and blue **Fuchs Palast**, a hotel designed by the painter Ernst Fuchs in an indescribable style which invites comparison with the idiosyncratic buildings of Friedensreich Hundertwasser.

View over Friesach

Far more important in earlier times than St Veit was little **Friesach**, guarding the ancient north-south trade route further north. The oldest town in Carinthia, it has kept its historic appearance virtually intact despite numerous sieges and fires, and can even boast a water-filled moat, a unique feature in German-speaking Europe.

The crypt of Gurk Cathedral

Aside from the main north-south route, the valley of the river Gurk heads into the hills to the west. Beyond the hilltop castle at **Strassburg** is the village of **Gurk**. This rather remote spot boasts the most important Romanesque church in Austria, a splendid twin-towered structure in pale stone built in the mid-12th century over a convent church founded a century earlier by Countess Emma, Carinthia's patron saint.

A 26km (16-mile) drive to the east of Strassburg lies **Hüttenberg** ⓮, a market town with one quite unique attraction – the **Heinrich Harrer Museum** (May–Oct daily 10am–5pm; charge). Harrer (1912–2006) was an Austrian climber, adventurer and writer, best known as the author of the book Seven Years in Tibet. The museum documents his life, his friendship with the Dalai Lama, his relationship with Tibet, and cultures that he experienced during his travels.

Villach and Ossiacher See

Known primarily as an important rail, main road and motorway junction close to border crossings with Italy and Slovenia, **Villach** is often overlooked by travellers in a hurry. But Carinthia's second-largest town is a handsome old place, worth

The arcaded courtyard of Schloss Porcia in Spittal an der Drau

more than a casual inspection even if you are not taking the thermal waters of the modern spa area, Warmbad Villach, just to the south. Sloping gently upwards from the bridge over the River Drau, the main square, Hauptplatz, has a spaciousness that contrasts with the inviting intimacy of the narrow alleyways opening off to either side. At the top of the square stands the stately parish church of St Jakob with a 95m (312ft) freestanding bell tower that can be climbed. Villach is within striking distance of several of Carinthia's lakes. The little **Faakersee** just to the east is popular with locals, and the resort of **Faak am See** has what is claimed to be Austria's largest and most lavishly landscaped model railway, the **Modellbahnparadies** (May, June, Sept Tue–Sun 1–6pm, July, Aug daily 10am–6pm, Oct Thur–Sun 1–5pm; charge). To the north, equally close, is Carinthia's third-largest lake, the **Ossiacher See**, as busy as the Wörthersee but rather less sophisticated. From Annenheim on the north shore, a gondola then a chair-lift whisk visitors up to the 1,909m (6,263ft) summit of the **Gerlitzen**, from where there is a fabulous panorama of lakes and mountains. In the village of **Ossiach** on the south shore stands the abbey of the same name. Its church has luscious stucco decoration, while its other buildings now house a hotel.

Drau Valley and Beyond

From Villach, rail and road head northwest, following the River Drau towards their respective tunnels through the Hohe Tauern mountains. They part company at **Spittal an der Drau**, an attractive old town whose name recalls its origins as a medieval *Spittal* or hospice for travellers on what has always been one of the main routes through the Alps. At the very centre of town is **Schloss Porcia**, a superb Renaissance palace with a three-storey arcaded courtyard which makes an atmospheric setting for a summer theatre festival. The palace's top floor and vast attics are home to the extensive and fascinating collections of the **Museum für Volkskultur** (Ethnographical Museum; mid-Apr–Oct Mon–Sat 9am–6pm; charge), arranged in themed displays (farm life, school room etc.). Spittal's local lake is the **Millstätter See**, Carinthia's second-largest (and deepest) body of water, with all the facilities to be expected. Resort villages are strung out along the sunny north shore, while the forested and shady southern shore remains almost entirely undeveloped. Dominating the village of **Millstatt** is its abbey, founded in the 11th century and still retaining some original features such as lovely Romanesque cloisters and a 1,000-year-old lime tree.

Just off the autobahn north of Spittal is the tiny medieval townlet of **Gmünd**, so perfectly preserved as to resemble a stage set. In this unlikely setting, just outside the town walls, is a temple to an icon of modern technology, the **Porsche Automuseum Helmut Pfeifhofer** (daily mid-May–mid-Oct 9am–6pm, mid-Oct–mid-May 10am–4pm; charge). The Porsche operation was evacuated to this remote spot during World

Heiligenblut

War II, and it was here that Ferdinand Porsche worked on the design of his legendary 356 model. Gmünd is the starting point for the **Malta-Hochalm-Strasse**, a spectacular panoramic toll road that climbs 1,000m (3,300ft) into the heart of the Tauern range past numerous waterfalls to one of the country's most awe-inspiring dams, an engineering triumph holding back the glacier-fed waters of the **Kölnbrein** reservoir.

To the west of Spittal, the Drau is joined by its important tributary, the Möll. A drive up its long and increasingly attractive valley, the **Mölltal**, leads into the very heart of the Hohe Tauern mountains and to one of the most memorable experiences of any visit to Austria, the spectacular panoramic road known as the **Grossglockner Hochalpenstrasse** (Grossglockner High Alpine Road; see page 104). Guarding the southern approach to the Grossglockner, the last village in Carinthia, **Heiligenblut ⓯**, is also one of the most photographed – the pencil-slim spire of its Gothic parish church harmonising perfectly with the glaciers and eternal snowfields beyond.

East Tyrol
More easily reached from Carinthia than from the provincial capital of Innsbruck, East Tyrol is nevertheless utterly

Tyrolean in heart and soul. Its inhabitants were particularly affected by the transfer of South Tyrol to Italy after World War I, since this cut the direct rail and road route to Innsbruck and the rest of the province. Improved relations with Italy and the construction in 1967 of the Felbertauern road tunnel to Mittersill in Salzburger Land have eased the situation, but East Tyrol still feels rather isolated from the mainstream. For the discriminating visitor this can be an advantage; while there is plenty to do and see here, the area is less overwhelmed by tourism than other parts of Austria, and much of it has a pleasantly old-fashioned feel. As well as winter sports in the valleys running south from the main ridge of the Alps, there's superb summer walking, with trails leading into the heart of the high mountains.

Overlooked by the dramatic limestone peaks of the Lienz Dolomites at the confluence of the Drau with the Isel, East Tyrol's principal town, historic **Lienz**, is well worth a stop off. As well as a handsome central square, alive in an almost Mediterranean way in summer with open-air cafes and restaurants, it has a splendid Stadtpfarrkirche. This richly furnished Gothic-Baroque parish church is surrounded by an arcaded churchyard, where a war memorial chapel is decorated with striking Expressionist paintings by the town's most revered son, Albin Egger-Lienz (1868–1926). More of the artist's work, including his famous depiction of a peasant mowing his field, can be seen in the local museum, housed in **Schloss Bruck** (mid-May–mid-Sept daily

The Lienz Dolomites

Lentos Kunstmuseum in Linz

10am–6pm, mid-Sept–Oct Tue–Sun 10am–4pm; charge)
just above the town.

UPPER AUSTRIA

Centred like Lower Austria on the great artery of the Danube,
Upper Austria tends to be slightly overlooked by visitors from
abroad. Its most popular tourist region, the glorious lakes and
mountains of the Salzkammergut, are shared with Salzburg
and Styria. But the province's dynamic capital, Linz, is worth
more than a casual visit, and there is plenty of unspoiled countryside, any number of small historic towns and some of the
country's greatest monastic foundations to be explored.

Linz

Astride the Danube as it widens into a broad valley, Austria's
third-largest city is a thriving centre of business, industry and

cultural innovation, quite capable of shrugging off its characterisation by snooty Viennese as a provincial backwater ('Linz ist Provinz!'), not least because of its 2009 role as a European City of Culture.

Linz's origins go back to Roman times, and its strategic position at the point where the old north-south salt route crossed the river guaranteed its prosperity in the Middle Ages. Its Schloss and its spacious **Hauptplatz**, one of the largest and finest historic town squares in Central Europe, date from this time. The city's industrial role really began after Austria's annexation by Nazi Germany in 1938, when the vast Hermann-Goering-Werke was built, the forerunner of today's chemical and steel plants. Hitler spent much of his adolescence here, and the city occupied a special place in his affections, though happily his megalomaniacal plans for its post-war transformation remained on paper, apart from the **Niebelungenbrücke**, the bridge linking the Altstadt with the suburb of **Urfahr** on the north bank of the Danube. Facing each other across the river are two striking contemporary building emblematic of the city's confidence in its cultural heritage and its willingness to embrace the technological future. Urfahr has the **Ars Electronica Center** (Tue, Wed, Fri 9am–5pm, Thur until 9pm, Sat–Sun 10am–6pm; charge). This temple devoted to the evolving age of electronic trickery and virtual reality offers an array of hands-on experiences guaranteed to amaze even the biggest technophobe. On the south bank, the **Lentos Kunstmuseum** (Tue–Sun 10am–6pm; charge) is home to an outstanding collection of 19th- and 20th-century art including masterpieces by Austrian greats such as Klimt, Schiele and Kokoschka. Close by is the concert hall named after Anton Bruckner (1824–95), the composer who had the closest associations with Linz, though the city is also proud that Mozart wrote his Symphony No.36 (the 'Linz') here in what is now the Mozarthaus in the Altstadt.

The fireman's saint

The patron saint of Linz and Upper Austria as well as of firefighters and chimney sweeps, St Florian was a Roman official who converted to Christianity. Refusing to sacrifice to pagan gods, in the year 304 he was condemned to death and thrown into the River Enns with a millstone round his neck. He is usually depicted as a Roman soldier attending to a burning building.

Linz makes a fine base for trips into the surrounding area, but the city-dwellers' favourite excursion is a climb up the local mountain, the **Pöstlingberg**, preferably by the little electric tramway which is claimed to be the steepest of its kind anywhere. As well as offering expansive views, the hilltop is crowned by a classic twin-towered Baroque pilgrimage church.

A trio of abbeys

Within easy reach of Linz are three of Austria's finest abbey complexes. A few kilometres upstream stands Cistercian **Stift Wilhering**, with a church interior in Rococo style whose exuberance almost defies description. Further away to the south-west of the city, the Benedictine abbey at **Kremsmünster** is supposed to have been founded as long ago as 777, on the spot where a Bavarian prince was killed while hunting boar. The present Baroque group of buildings date from the late 17th century, and, as well as a typically sumptuous church interior, include a massive 50m (165ft) -high observatory and a unique set of ornamental carp ponds. To the southeast of Linz, the largest and most visited of these abbeys is the Augustinian **Stift St Florian** ⑯, at the terminus of a now-defunct tram-line from the city. The organ of the glorious Baroque abbey church is named after Bruckner, who was a chorister and organist here and who is buried beneath it. The abbey interiors (May–Sept daily; guided tours at 11am, 1pm, 3pm; charge) include the superbly panelled Library, a Marble Hall, Imperial Apartments, and the largest collection anywhere of paintings by Albrecht Altdorfer (1480–1538), whose gift for combining the drama of biblical scenes with dynamic Danubian landscapes is plain to see.

Beyond St Florian, on the banks of the River Enns just before it flows into the Danube, is the pretty little walled town of **Enns**. Equally charming, on the far side of the Danube, is the village of Mauthausen, known however not for its attractiveness but as the site of one of the most notorious Nazi concentration camps, **KZ Mauthausen** (daily 9am–5.30pm; charge). The horrors perpetrated here are remembered in the displays of the visitor centre while several memorials commemorate those who suffered and perished.

Steyr

In its heyday in the late Middle Ages, this old industrial town at the confluence of the Rivers Enns and Steyr was the most prosperous in Austria, with a key location on the 'Iron Road' leading north from the ore mines of Eisenerz in Styria. Industry still flourishes, but Steyr's Altstadt is nevertheless one of the loveliest in Austria; its centrepiece is the Hauptplatz, a long main square hemmed with fine old houses including the famous Bummerlhaus, a Gothic courtyard edifice dating from 1497. Music-lovers will be interested to learn that

Kremsmünster Abbey at sunset

Schubert was captivated by Steyr when he came on a visit, subsequently spending a whole year here during which he wrote his Trout Quintet. The town has an unusual and fascinating modern attraction, the **Museum Industrielle Arbeitswelt** (Working World Museum; Tue–Sun 9am–5pm; charge), consisting of a wealth of exhibits and interactive displays on the implications of galloping globalisation.

The Mühlviertel

This quiet upland corner of Austria lies between the Danube and the densely forested area along the Czech and Bavarian borders. A little train winds its leisurely way northwest from Linz to the double town of **Aigen-Schlägl**, the latter with a fine abbey church. Beyond, a long-distance trail leads towards the summit of the **Plöckenstein** (1,378m/4,524ft), close to the point where the three countries meet. North from Linz, the ancient trade route to Prague is much busier. It leads past **Kefermarkt**, where the church houses a huge and magnificent altar carved from limewood, to **Freistadt**. The unofficial capital of the Mühlviertel, this perfectly preserved little town has kept most of its fortifications, its two gateways, and a network of charming lanes focusing on a main square graced by fine old medieval houses with Baroque facades.

Inside Kefermarkt church

THE SALZKAMMERGUT

Shared by the provinces of Upper Austria, Salzburg and Styria, the Salzkammergut is one of Austria's most popular holiday regions, its myriad

A guesthouse on Wolfgangsee

lakes set splendidly in deep valleys between the alpine foothills and the jagged peaks of the mighty Dachstein. Its name reflects the age-old significance of its salt industry, still active today, though far outweighed by the importance of tourism which dates from the early 19th century, when the rich and famous began to come here to benefit from the health-restoring waters as well as from the incomparable scenery.

Bad Ischl

In a central position in the Salzkammergut, this busy spa town has easy access to the region's attractions and, with a variety of accommodation, is an obvious place to base yourself. This is certainly how it appeared to the Imperial family, who started to take the saline waters here in the early 19th century, thereby ensuring its fashionable status. A creature of habit, Emperor Franz Joseph spent every summer holiday in **Bad Ischl** ⓱ after becoming engaged to the beautiful

Sissi here in 1853. The hotel where he proposed is now the town museum, which understandably makes much of the Imperial connection, but the real draw for fans of royalty is the **Kaiservilla** (daily Apr, Oct 10am–4pm, May–Sept 9.30am–5pm, Jan–Mar Wed only 10am–4pm; charge). In its English-style park, this is a grand affair; but equally fascinating and more typical of the town is the **Lehárvilla** (May–Sept Wed–Sun 10am–5pm; charge), the summer residence of Franz Lehár (1870–1948) who composed many of his delightfully frothy operettas here.

Wolfgangsee and Mondsee

To the west of Bad Ischl, and within easy reach of Salzburg, are two of the region's most popular lakes, each with water that warms to a balmy temperature in summer. On the sunny northern shore of the 10km (6-mile) -long **Wolfgangsee** ⓲ stands the little picture-postcard town of **St Wolfgang**, known for the *Weisses Rössl*, the White Horse Inn which gave its name to the famous comic opera. Beautifully sited on a terrace above the lake, the parish church possesses a magnificent Late Gothic 12m (39ft) -high altarpiece, the work of the Tyrolean master carver Michael Pacher. The favourite excursion from St Wolfgang is by old-fashioned rack and pinion railway to the 1,785m (5,855ft) summit of the **Schafberg**, a splendid viewpoint taking in much of the Salzkammergut.

Windsurfing on Wolfgangsee

There are more panoramic views from the 1,521m (4,990ft) peak of the **Zwölferhorn** on the opposite shore of the lake, reached

Mozart fountain, St Gilgen

by cableway from **St Gilgen**. A pleasant resort town at the northwestern extremity of the lake, St Gilgen is proud of its associations with Mozart, whose mother was born here. With its beaches and sailing schools, the curving 11km (7-mile) -long **Mondsee** draws water-sports enthusiasts in large numbers. In the distant past it attracted Neolithic people whose dwellings rose from the lake on stilts, while much later, in the 8th century, it was the site of an early Benedictine monastery in what is now the little town of Mondsee. Successor to the monastery, the Baroque parish church with its array of superb altars entered the wider world's consciousness when it was the scene of the wedding in *The Sound of Music*.

Attersee and Traunsee

The largest lake not only in the Salzkammergut but in Austria as a whole, and ice-free in winter, the **Attersee** stretches for 20km (12 miles) from the highlands around the Schafberg in the south towards the industrial town of Lenzing in the gentler, undulating country to the north. A century ago, Gustav Mahler came to Steinbach on the eastern shore to compose his symphonies, while the painter Gustav Klimt favoured the southern end of the lake. Nowadays the lakeside villages are frequented mostly by devotees of water-based sports.

To the east, **Traunsee** is the country's deepest lake, with a partly inaccessible eastern shore beneath the rocky summit of the **Traunstein** (1,691m/5,548ft). From the salt-processing town of **Ebensee** in the south, a scenic road runs along the western shore, bypassing the pretty village of **Traunkirchen** on its promontory. The Baroque parish church here has a real treasure in the shape of its Fischerkanzel, a boat-shaped pulpit depicting the Miraculous Draught of Fishes in exuberant detail. At the northern extremity of the lake, **Gmunden** is an attractive and substantial historic town and resort, known for its salt-water cures, its ceramics and the decidedly offbeat **Klo & So Sanitärmuseum** (May, Sept Wed–Sun 10am–5pm, June–Aug Tue–Sun 10am–5pm; charge). 'Klo' means 'loo', and the museum boasts more than 300 porcelain items of lavatorial interest. Gmunden's promenade leads to a timber bridge giving access to the picturesque 17th-century **Seeschloss Ort**. On its island in the lake, the castle plays a leading role in *Schlosshotel Orth*, an extremely popular German TV soap, and consequently attracts viewers in large numbers.

Hallstatt

With its pretty pastel-coloured buildings crammed in between the deep and dark green waters of **Hallstätter See** and the precipitous slope of the mountain to the west, the village of **Hallstatt** ⑲ is deservedly world-famous. Bypassed by a road tunnel, and with its centre pleasantly traffic free, its appeal

Hallstätter See in the winter

can best be appreciated by approaching it aboard the ferry from the railway station on the far side of the lake. But not only is Hallstatt picturesque in the extreme, the spectacular archaeological finds made here in the 19th century led to its name being given to the highly developed Iron Age 'Hallstatt Culture' which flourished between 800 and 500BC. Even before this, salt was being extracted from the deposits above the village and brine is still pumped from here to be processed at Ebensee.

An array of fascinating Iron Age finds are beautifully presented in the **Museum** (daily Apr, Oct 10am–4pm, May–Sept 10am–6pm, Nov–Mar Wed–Sun 11am–3pm; charge), while high above the village and reached by funicular is **Salzwelten Hallstatt** (daily May–mid-Sept 9.30am–4.30pm, mid–late Sept 9.30am–3.30pm, Oct 9.30am–3pm; charge), an underground saltworks offering some exciting experiences including whizzing down into the depths of the mine by slide.

Inside Salzwelten Hallstatt

A cable-car ride from Obertraun at the far end of the lake up to the **Krippenstein** (2,110m/6,920ft) provides fabulous views over the southern flank of the Dachstein. From the halfway station there is access to the **Dachstein Caves**, among the region's most visited attractions and some of the largest glacial caves in the world. They include the **Mammuthöhle** (daily late May to late Oct 9.30am–3pm; charge) hollowed out of limestone, and the even more spectacular ice caves of the **Rieseneishöhle** (daily May–mid-Oct 8.30am–4pm; charge) with subterranean glaciers and frozen waterfalls.

Bad Aussee

Its early prosperity based on salt mining, Stryian Aussee added 'Bad' to its name when fashionable folk started to take the waters here in the early 19th century. Among them was the liberal-minded Archduke Johann who endeared himself to the populace by marrying the daughter of the local postmaster. Town life now centres on the modern spa complex and on the main square, which is graced by a fountain, a plague column and the splendid Gothic-cum-Renaissance **Kammerhof**, once the headquarters of the salt industry and now the local museum.

With no lake of its own, Bad Aussee is within easy reach of **Grundlsee** and **Altausseer See**. From Grundlsee, 6km (4 miles) long, there is a popular excursion by boat and on foot taking in two smaller water bodies as well: first, in a particularly rugged mountain setting, comes **Toplitzsee**, where the Nazis dumped quantities of forged British banknotes; and at the far end, through the woods, lies the tiny and idyllic **Kammersee**. Altausser See can be walked around in a couple of hours from the charming resort of Altaussee. Nearby is another show mine, the **Salzwelten Altaussee** (daily May, mid-Sept–Oct 9am–3pm, June–mid-Sept 9am–4pm; charge) whose underground chambers were used in World War II as a depository for artworks from all over occupied Europe. A scenic toll road zigzags up from Altauseeto to the mountain hut below the summit of the 1,837m (6,022ft) **Loser**, from where there are superb views over lakes and mountains.

SALZBURG AND SALZBURGER LAND

Salzburg and the province of which it is the capital offer complementary pleasures. The city is a high point of any visit to Austria, its sublime architectural heritage and its sophisticated

A boat celebrating Altaussee narcissus festival

Salzburg: the river, the city and the fortress

cultural life attracting cosmopolitan crowds from all over the globe. By contrast, the valleys and mountains of the *Land* (region) preserve many rustic traditions as well as being an all-year-round paradise for lovers of the great outdoors.

Salzburg

Straddling the Salzach river as it emerges from the Alpine foothills, the city of **Salzburg** ❷⓿ is a glorious fusion of nature, architecture, history and culture. Nature has provided the swiftly running river as well as the dramatic heights later crowned by citadels and churches. Powerful and ambitious prince-bishops embellished the close-knit medieval city in Renaissance and Baroque times in a bid to transform it into an Alpine Rome. More recently, Mozart heritage has inspired a cultural life that reaches its climax in the world-renowned Salzburg Festival. More recently still, *The Sound of Music* put the city on the map for many who might otherwise have never heard of it. Hardly a surprise then that Salzburg has become one of the world's great tourist destinations, with millions of visitors annually.

The Altstadt

At the foot of the hill known as the Mönchsberg, the alleyways, streets and charming arcaded courtyards of the older part of the city are laid out around its main thoroughfare, traffic-free **Getreidegasse** **Ⓐ**. Among the tall, narrow-fronted old houses with their wrought-iron shop signs is **Mozarts Geburtshaus** (daily July–Aug 9am–8pm, Sept–June 9am–5.30pm; charge), where the composer was born in 1756 and wrote many of his earliest works. Heaps of Mozart memorabilia fill the house including instruments used by the infant genius. Curving Judengasse leads into Mozartplatz, one of a sequence of squares at the eastern end of the Altstadt. Of these the grandest is **Residenzplatz**, with a superb fountain at its centre. On one side is the north flank of the cathedral, on another the **Residenz** itself (daily 10am–5pm; charge), begun in 1595 by the most flamboyant of Salzburg's rulers, Archbishop Wolf Dietrich, though much of the opulent decor of its state apartments dates from the 18th century. Beyond is Domplatz, overlooked by the grandiose twin-towered west front of the **Dom**, the cathedral intended by Wolf Dietrich to be a rival to Rome's St Peter's. It was completed, albeit scaled down, by his marginally less spendthrift successors. Another fine fountain, in fact an over-the-top horse trough, forms the focal point of Kapitelplatz, the square to the south of the cathedral, while to the west, nudging the

Residenzplatz fountain

cliff rising to the Mönchsberg, the **Peterskirche** contradicts its austere outward appearance with a gloriously ostentatious Rococo interior. Its churchyard has catacombs hewn into the cliff by the early Christian inhabitants of Juvavum, Salzburg's Roman predecessor. Further west still, on Max Reinhard Platz, is the **Rupertium** (Tue–Sun 10am–6pm; charge), a gallery with works by Klimt and Kokoschka, and beyond, the **Festspielhaus**, the principal venue of the Salzburg Festival.

The Mönchsberg

Rising some 120m (400ft) above town and river, the Mönchsberg provided an easily defensible site when the archbishops decided to build themselves a fortress. Reached swiftly by funicular, the **Hohensalzburg ❸** (daily May–Sept 9am–7pm, Oct–Apr 9.30am–5pm; charge includes funicular) was begun in the 11th century. It's an intriguing ensemble of buildings and interiors of various dates, including state apartments added around 1500, which have retained many of their original furnishings and decor. At the western end of the heights, an uncompromisingly modern addition to Salzburg's

The Salzburg Festival

Staged annually in July and August at a variety of spectacular locations, this is one of the key events in the international music festival calendar, attracting the cream of the world's talent. Inaugurated in 1920 by Salzburg's great theatre director Max Reinhard, the composer Richard Strauss and the playwright Hugo von Hofmannsthal, it emerged from the city's growing appreciation of its greatest son, Mozart, whom it had neglected for many years. In the years following World War II, the figure most closely identified with the festival was the conductor Herbert von Karajan (1908–89), whose almost demonic energy not only revitalised it, but helped overshadow his former membership of the Nazi Party.

architectural wealth is the **Museum der Moderne** (Tue–Sun 9am–6pm; charge), housing changing exhibitions of contemporary art.

Right Bank
The equivalent of Getreidegasse on the far bank of the Salzach is busy **Linzergasse**, while the Mönchsberg is replicated by the **Kapuzinerberg**, named after the Capuchin church at the summit. Fine views over the city open up from here, while another

Salzburg Dom

classic vista can be enjoyed from Salzburg's loveliest park, the glorious formal gardens of **Schloss Mirabell**. Now housing administrative offices and much modified, the Schloss was originally built by Archbishop Wolf Dietrich for Salome Alt, his mistress and the mother of his many children. Complementing Mozart's birthplace in the Altstadt is the **Mozarts-Wohnhaus** (daily July–Aug 9am–8pm, Sept–June 9am–5.30pm; charge), where the composer lived between 1773 and 1780. Excellent multimedia displays more than compensate for a relative lack of original memorabilia here.

Schloss Hellbrunn
Just to the south of the city, the Baroque **Schloss Hellbrunn** ㉑ (daily July–Aug 9am–6pm, May–June, Sept 9am–5.30pm, Apr, Oct 9am–4.30pm; charge) was commissioned in 1615 by Archbishop Marcus Sitticus as his country retreat. The guests of this worldly prelate would be lavishly entertained in the palace's sumptuous interiors, then amused by a stroll

through the **gardens** with their extraordinary array of water features, including suddenly spurting fountains which still spray unwary visitors today. Hellbrunn is also the location of Salzburg's **zoo** and the **Volkskundemuseum** with fascinating displays on the province's rich folk traditions.

Along the Salzach

Running south from Salzburg, the valley of the Salzach gives access to the Alpine districts of the province, still referred to by their traditional '-gau' names (Pinzgau, Pongau etc). Much of the wealth of the Salzburg archbishops came from the salt mines of the attractive old town of **Hallein**, though the 'white gold' had been worked long before, notably by the Celtic inhabitants of the area. The history of salt mining and the Celtic past are expounded in the **Keltenmuseum** (Apr–Oct daily 9am–5pm; charge) and in the reconstructed settlement called the

Schloss Hellbrunn

Keltendorf (daily Apr–Oct 9am–5pm, Nov–Mar 11am–3pm; charge) in the village of Bad Dürrnberg above the town. Here too there is a show mine, **Salzwelten Salzburg** ㉒ (same opening times; charge), offering a sequence of exciting experiences including the traditional whizz down a timber slide, plus an underground train ride and boat trip.

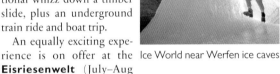
Ice World near Werfen ice caves

An equally exciting experience is on offer at the **Eisriesenwelt** (July–Aug 9.30am–4.30pm, May–June, Sept–Oct 9.30am–3.30pm; charge), high above the village of Werfen and reached by road and cable car. These are some of the most extensive and spectacular ice caves anywhere, made even more dramatic when lit only by the lamps of guides and visitors. On a rocky outcrop far below stands the impregnable-looking crag-top fortress of **Hohenwerfen**, built by the archbishops in the 11th century.

Upstream from the garrison town and ski centre of **St Johann im Pongau**, the Salzach valley turns westwards towards the river's source on the border with Tyrol. Most of its tributaries originate in the mighty **Hohe Tauern** mountains to the south, much of which is protected as a national park shared between Salzburg, Tyrol and Carinthia. One side stream, the Grossarl, approaches the Salzach in the dramatically narrow gorge of the **Liechtensteinklamm**, in part barely 2m (6ft) wide and hemmed in by 300m (1,000ft) cliffs.

Badgastein

The most important side valley joining the Salzach from the south is the **Gasteinertal**, the route followed by the strategic Tauernbahn trans-Alpine railway opened in 1905. A few kilometres short of the entrance to the rail tunnel through the Hohe Tauern, the spa resort of **Badgastein** is laid out in a spectacular mountain setting around the waterfalls of the Gasteiner Ache. The healing properties of the area's thermal, lightly radioactive waters had been known for hundreds of years, but the spa only became fashionable in the 19th century when it enjoyed Habsburg patronage and attracted a glittering international clientele. Badgastein still exudes something of the atmosphere of that time, though nowadays as many visitors come here for the first-rate winter sports and summer hiking as for the cure, which can be taken in hotels, in the spa itself or deep in tunnels bored into the mountainside.

The Pinzgau

Known as the Pinzgau, the upper valley of the Salzach has as its miniature capital the charming old town of **Zell-am-See** ㉓, idyllically located on the west bank of the Zeller See, one of the loveliest and (in summer) warmest of the Austria's mountain lakes. Zell has joined with the resorts of **Saalbach** to the west and **Kaprun** a few kilometres to the south to form the so-called Europa Sportregion, with an impressive choice of all-year recreational facilities; on a summer day it is quite feasible to combine skiing on the glaciers above Kaprun in the morning with an afternoon swim in the Zeller See.

The classic excursion from Zell is by cableway to the top of the local mountain, the **Schmittenhöhe** (1,964m/6,445ft), which offers fabulous all-round views, including the snowy peaks of the Hohe Tauern away to the south. There are even

Chairlifts over Zell am See

more extensive views from the top station (3,029m/9,938ft) of the three-stage cableway which climbs nearly to the summit of the 3,203m (10,508ft) **Kitzsteinhorn** from Kaprun; with a guide, the reasonably fit can conquer the peak itself as well as taking a walk on the glacier. A very different kind of excursion starts from the Kesselfall Alpenhaus a short distance up the valley from Kaprun. A combination of buses and funicular gives access to the **Wasserfallboden** and **Mooserboden**, two of the most dramatically sited hydroelectric reservoirs in the Alps.

The northern Pinzgau to the north of Zell-am-See is also well worth exploring. Here the dramatic peaks forming the border with Bavaria's Berchtesgadener Land rise steeply above the valley, the great limestone plateau of the **Steinernes Meer** (Sea of Stone) culminating in the imposing massif of the **Hochkönig** (2,940m/9,650ft). The base of the mountain can be reached by following the road between **Bischofshofen** and Saalfelden; from **Mühlbach** you can drive directly up to the Arthurhaus (1,500m/ 4,925ft) by car. **Maria Alm am Steinernen Meer** is a pretty place along the route; the parish and pilgrimage church, which dates from around 1500, has the highest spire in Salzburger Land (85m/275ft). The administrative centre of **Saalfelden** is home to the **Pinzgau Museum of Local History** in Ritzen Castle (1604), which contains, along with other exhibits, the largest collection of Christmas cribs in Austria.

Grossglockner

To the east of Kaprun, an ancient trading route follows the valley of the Fuscher Ache southwards into the heart of the Hohe Tauern and the **Grossglockner Hochalpenstrasse** ❷❹ (High Alpine Road). Celtic, Roman and medieval remains

The winding Grossglockner Hochalpenstrasse

found along its course testify to the importance of
the old pass route which
traversed the Alps to the
east of the Grossglockner,
Austria's highest peak
(3,797m/12,461ft). But it
was only in the early 1930s,
with the urgent need to
relieve some of the coun-
try's acute unemployment,
that this gloriously scenic,
meticulously engineered

Krimmler Wasserfälle

toll highway was laid out. Forty-eight kilometres (30 miles)
in length, and with 27 hairpin bends, it connects Salzburger
Land with Carinthia, reaching its summit at Hochtor
(2,504m/8,215ft) and passing numerous information points
along the way. A narrow side road climbs even higher to
the Edelweiss Peak (2,571m/8,435ft), while another diversion leads to the route's main attraction, the **Kaiser-Franz-
Josephs-Höhe**, with an array of visitor facilities and a
commanding view of the spectacular Pasterze Glacier and
the Grossglockner itself.

Back in the Salzach valley, the old town of Mittersill is the
starting point of another old pass route, superseded since
the 1960s by the 5km (3-mile) -long **Felber-Tauern Tunnel**,
which pierces the main ridge of the Alps between Austria's
highest (Grossglockner) and second-highest (Grossvenediger:
3,674m/12,050ft) mountains. At the end of the valley, before
the road starts its climb over the Gerlos Pass into Tyrol, the
waters of the Salzach crash down in a series of falls, the
Krimmler Wasserfälle ㉕ (Apr–Oct; charge), one of the
country's great natural wonders, unequalled anywhere else in
the Alps.

TYROL

Innsbruck folklore on parade

Straddling one of the main routes between northern Europe and Italy, Austria's third-largest province has a long and proud tradition of offering hospitality to travellers. But rather than passing through, today's visitors come to stay, revelling in what many consider to be the country's finest alpine scenery, a classic mixture of rugged peaks, shining glaciers, verdant valleys, rushing rivers and cheerful villages. Tyrolean towns too are of exceptional interest, from historic little places like Hall to the mountain-girdled capital Innsbruck. The locals are also a special bunch, with a strong sense of history and local identity that expresses itself in the everyday wearing of traditional dress and the enthusiastic observance of old customs.

Innsbruck

More than Austria's other provincial capitals, **Innsbruck** ㉖ is a truly Alpine city. The fast-flowing, milky-green waters of the River Inn have a highland turbulence about them; immediately to the north rises the massive southern wall of the Karwendelgebirge range which forms the border with Bavaria, while to the south the road to the Brenner Pass is flanked by ever more imposing heights, the snowfields and glaciers of the

Zillertaler Alps to the east, the Ötztaler Alps to the west. Not particularly large, Innsbruck has direct access to its glorious surroundings, where a garland of pretty villages offer summer hiking and winter sports; the city is proud of the fact that its office workers can nip up to the slopes for a quick spot of lunch-hour skiing. The compact, traffic-free historic centre is a delight to explore, and Innsbruck as a whole exudes a powerful, distinctly Tyrolean identity.

The city centre

Innsbruck's main thoroughfare is the broad Maria Theresien Strasse which runs south from the Altstadt, the city's medieval core, to the **Triumphpforte**, a triumphal arch commemorating the marriage of Empress Maria Theresa's son Leopold to the Infanta of Spain in 1765. Halfway along its length, the street frames one of the most photographed vistas in Austria, in the foreground the Baroque victory column called the **Annasäule**, in the background the often snowcapped Karwendel heights. Defined by the ring road (Marktgraben, Burggraben) laid out along the line of the old moat, Innsbruck's Altstadt consists of a web of narrow lanes and streets, some lined with arcaded medieval houses buttressed against earthquakes.

Taking a break in Innsbruck

Herzog-Friedrich-Strasse leads to the famous **Goldenes Dachl** , an ornate loggia attached to the otherwise plain ducal palace by Emperor Maximilian I around 1500. From the balcony roofed with gilded copper tiles the emperor could

View over Innsbruck

greet his subjects gathered in the square below. Inside the building, the **Museum Goldenes Dachl** (May–Sept daily 10am–5pm, Oct–Apr Tue–Sun 10am–5pm; charge) tells the story of this member of the Habsburg dynasty who brought Innsbruck brief fame as the imperial capital. Nearby, the tall **Stadtturm** (daily June–Sept 10am–8pm, Oct–May 10am–5pm; charge) can be climbed for a bird's-eye view of the city and its dramatic setting.

To the north are the 18th century **Domkirche** (Cathedral) and the **Hofburg**, once the seat of the court. More fascinating than either is the **Hofkirche** ❽ (Mon–Sat 9am–5pm, Sun 12.30–5pm; charge), a mostly Gothic structure whose great treasure is the extraordinary **Grabmal Kaiser Maximilians I** (Mausoleum of Emperor Maximilian I). Based on Maximilian's own designs, this supreme example of Early Renaissance sculpture features an array of larger-than-life figures representing his (hypothetical) ancestors, among them English King Arthur. Next door, the **Tiroler Volkskunstmuseum** (Folklore Museum; daily 9am–5pm; charge) is the most comprehensive of its kind in Austria, a treasure house of traditional Alpine life. In the nearby **Ferdinandeum** (Provincial Museum of Tyrol; Tue–Sun daily 9am-5pm; charge), the most fascinating section is devoted to Tyrolean art, where the outstanding figure is the 15th-century master-carver Michael Pacher, the creator of many fabulous altarpieces.

Beyond the Altstadt

One of the most exciting things to do in Innsbruck is to take a ride on the rebuilt **Hungerbergbahn.** With structures designed by the internationally acclaimed architect Zaha Hadid, this funicular railway whizzes passengers from the Congress Centre just north of the Hofburg, across the Inn, and up the Hungerberg mountain (900m/2,950ft). An intermediate station serves the city zoo. Further cable cars give access to Hafelekar (2,334m/7,658ft) high up on the Karwendel ridge with stunning views of the Inn valley in its Alpine setting.

Anyone wanting to learn about Tyrol's intriguing past should visit the old imperial arsenal, the **Zeughaus** (daily 9am–5pm; charge), with excellent displays on such subjects as the province's early 19th-century struggle for independence led by the archetypal Tyrolean hero, Andreas Hofer.

Hofer's battles were fought on the **Bergisel** hill on the southern edge of the city, just above the suburb of **Wilten**

Andreas Hofer

In 1809, this innkeeper and publican raised the banner of revolt against the French and their Bavarian allies. The forced annexation of the Tyrol to Bavaria was bad enough, but what really outraged the conservative Tyroleans was the introduction of progressive reforms such as religious tolerance. Astonishingly, Hofer's ragged peasant army managed to defeat its well-armed, professional adversaries not once, but three times. Finally, however, superior force prevailed; with no support from Vienna, Hofer's men were defeated. Their leader fled, was betrayed, and suffered execution by a French firing squad.

Nearly two centuries after his death, the bushy-bearded, black-hatted rebel still enjoys great popularity among traditionally minded Tyroleans (a majority), though his cult is sniped at by sceptics (a tiny minority), who have provocatively compared him and his fanatical followers to the Taliban.

with its massive basilica and abbey church. The great man is honoured by a statue as well as at the **Kaiserjägermuseum** (daily 9am–5pm; charge), which celebrates the exploits of Hofer's men and those of the Tyrolean Imperial Regiments.

In the southeastern part of the city is the splendid palace known as **Schloss Ambras** (daily 10am–5pm; charge). It was given its Renaissance character when it was the seat of Archduke Ferdinand II, the great Maximilian's grandson. Famous for his marriage to a beautiful commoner, Ferdinand was an avid collector of art and objects of all kinds, particularly those of a grotesque character, and a fascinating selection of his 'cabinet of curiosities' is on show here.

Stunning views along the Brenner Pass

Brenner Pass

From Innsbruck, a main road, a trunk rail line (opened 1867) and a motorway (completed 1969) lead to the **Brenner Pass** (1,375m/4,510ft), about 40km (25 miles) to the south. The motorway passes over the 190m (625ft) **Europabrücke**, for many years the highest bridge of its kind on the continent and today a popular bungee jumping location.

To either side of the main valley are attractive mountain villages such as **Igls**, the site of the 1964 and 1976 Winter

Olympics. The lowest crossing of the Alps and one of the busiest, the Brenner marks the watershed between rivers feeding the Danube and eventually the Black Sea and those discharging into the Mediterranean. The best diversion from the main route leads up the **Stubaital** to the southwest. The valley's villages nearly all boast fine churches built in the 18th century by a local parish priest, Franz da Paula Penze, but most visitors come here less for the architecture than for skiing on the Stubai glacier.

East Along the Inn

A string of fine old towns follows the valley of the Inn downstream, many of them built on the proceeds of medieval salt and silver mining. Outstanding among them, within sight of Innsbruck, is **Hall**. The town's small and beautifully preserved historic core is built on rising ground a short distance north of the river, its focal point the **Oberer Stadtplatz**. The buildings around the irregularly shaped square testify to Hall's late medieval golden age when it was one of Austria's foremost cities. Prominent edifices include the steep-roofed Rathaus and the stately parish church, famous for its many saintly relics.

South Tyrol/Alto Adige

Until 1919 the Brenner linked rather than separated North, South and East Tyrol. But in that year South Tyrol was given to Italy, a thank you present from the Allies for having come in on their side in World War I. This wrecked the unity of Tyrol; not only was the South – in many ways the Tyrolean heartland – lost, but the East was cut off from the rest of the province. Attempts to Italianise what was now called 'Alto Adige' created bad blood between Austria and Italy, both before and after World War II, but since the granting of autonomy to the province in 1992 the situation has eased.

On lower ground, built to command the river crossing, is the 13th-century stronghold of **Burg Hasegg** (Apr–Oct Tue–Sun 10am–5pm, Nov, Dec, late Mar Tue–Sat 10am–5pm; charge). Its past role as Tyrol's mint is entertainingly communicated in its interactive displays. It was here that the first Taler coin, from which the word 'dollar' comes, was struck. At the nearby village of Wattens, a world-famous manufacturer of cut-glass objects has established the extremely popular **Swarovski Kristallwelten** (daily 9am–6.30pm; charge), with an array of ingenious and ultra-sophisticated installations demonstrating what can be done with crystal. Silver mining flourished at **Schwaz**, making it a rival to Hall; one of the old mines is now open to the public. At exquisite little **Rattenberg** the ore ran out as early as the 17th century; growth stopped, leaving it as one of the smallest towns in Austria with a population of just a few hundred. Glassware is a theme here too, with a works turning out an array of colourful items.

Astride the Inn just before it flows into Germany, **Kufstein** is dominated by its great **Festung** (daily Apr–Oct 9am–5pm, Nov–Mar 10am–4pm; charge), the medieval citadel strengthened by Emperor Maximilian when he wrested the town from the hands of the Bavarians in 1504; **Kaiserturm** – the massive, cylindrical tower erected on his orders – has walls 7.5m (25ft) thick. Equally gigantic in its proportions is the **Heldenorgel**, the largest organ in the world, installed here in 1931 to commemorate the dead of World War I.

Kitzbühel

Kufstein is one gateway to the jagged limestone peaks of the **Kaisergebirge**, the town of **St Johann in Tirol** in the broad valley at the eastern end of the range is another. There are plenty of smaller winter and summer resorts scattered around, but the undisputed star of this whole recreational region in northeastern Tyrol is glamorous **Kitzbühel**. Once a copper

Cable car from Maurach

and silver-mining town, and still with a couple of attractive old streets lined with typical old Tyrolean houses, Kitzbühel has made its modern fortune from winter sports. Skiing began in the late 19th century, the prestigious Hahnenkamm race in 1931. The gentle, rounded Kitzbühel Alps provide dozens of runs as well as relatively undemanding summer walking and cycling, while the bars and boutiques of the town offer plenty of glitz at all times.

Achensee and Zillertal

High above the town of Jenbach in the valley of the Inn, flanked by the Karwendel mountains to the west and the Rofan range to the east, the 10km (6-mile) -long **Achensee** is Tyrol's largest and loveliest lake, attracting holiday-makers and water sports enthusiasts in great numbers. A road winds up from Jenbach, though a jollier alternative is to take one of the veteran steam trains of the rack-and-pinion Achenseebahn which climbs up to the village of **Maurach** near the southern end of the lake. From Jenbach, another steam train, as well as more frequent diesels, runs the length of the **Zillertal**, deservedly one of the most popular and most developed of Austria's Alpine valleys.

An excellent way to appreciate the valley in its spectacular mountain setting is to turn off the main road on to the **Zillertaler Höhenstrasse**, the sometimes steep and narrow toll road which winds up to a height of 2,020m (6,628ft) on the western flank of the valley. One of the road's starting points is from **Zell am Ziller**, at the foot of the 1,507m (4,944ft) Gerlos Pass linking Tyrol to Salzburger Land. As its name implies, Zell has its origins in the cell of a monk, who arrived here in the 8th century on a mission to Christianise the region. The town has a fine late 18th-century church on an octagonal plan, but is perhaps better known for the beery Gauderfest

Hiking near Mayrhofen

held at the beginning of May. Towards the head of the Zillertal, where the main valley splits into four, known as 'Gründe', stands **Mayrhofen**, a busy summer and winter resort with plenty of facilities. From the town itself, mountain pastures and a network of hiking paths are quickly reached by using the Ahornbahn cable car, while

other rewarding excursions are to be made by exploring the Gründe. The upper reaches of most of them are only accessible on foot, though private cars are allowed up the Zamsergrund to the banks of the dramatically sited Schlegeis reservoir at 1,800m (5,906ft). From here, keen walkers can hike in about two hours to the chalet on the border with Italy (passport may be required). The most thrilling trip, however, is from the year-round ski resort of **Hintertux** at the head of the **Tuxer Grund**. From here a three-stage cableway takes skiers and trippers up to a viewing terrace above the Hintertux glacier at 3,250m (10,663ft). The awesome prospect ranges from the Dolomites in the south to the Zugspitze in the north.

Seefeld and the Zugspitze

The road from Innsbruck to Garmisch-Partenkirchen in Bavaria gives access to a high-level plateau bounded by the austere peaks of the Karwendel, Mieminger and Wetterstein ranges. With a privileged location among the attractive forests and pastures of the plateau is **Seefeld**, one of Austria's leading Alpine resorts. Host town to the Nordic skiing events during the 1964 and 1976 Olympics, this much-favoured summer and winter destination prides itself on combining a cosy village

Beautiful scenery in the Ötztal

atmosphere with that of a sophisticated tourist metropolis. The cross-country skiing facilities are outstanding, with more than 250km (155 miles) of well-maintained *loipen* (trails). One local landmark is the delightful little circular Baroque church known as the Seekirchl, much photographed against its mountain setting. Another is the lovely 15th-century Gothic parish church, dedicated to the Northumbrian martyr St Oswald.

At the western extremity of the Wetterstein range and right on the border with Bavaria, the **Zugspitze** ㉗ (2,962m/9,718ft) may not match up to Austria's Grossglockner in height, but Germany's highest peak is far more accessible. Cableways on both sides of the frontier whisk visitors up to the summit's viewing platforms in minutes, from where in clear weather there are stupendous views over Alpine peaks in four countries. The valley station of the Austrian **Zugspitzbahn** (May–Oct, Dec–mid-Apr; passport required) is in Obermoos, a short distance from the resort village of **Ehrwald**.

South of the Inn

Of all the valleys running south from the Inn, the **Ötztal** is the longest and perhaps the most fascinating. Narrow ravines alternate with broad, fertile basins as the valley climbs in a series of steps formed by the action of ancient glaciers. The upper valley is dominated by the snowy peaks and ice fields of the **Ötztaler Alpen**, Tyrol's highest mountains, and traditionally the Ötztal had closer links with South Tyrol than with the Inn valley; even today, shepherds drive their flocks northwards across the border to graze here in summer. The valley has much to attract visitors: the romantic little **Piburger See** is Tryol's warmest lake, the **Stuibenfälle** are splendid 150m (492ft) waterfalls, and there is superlative skiing and summer hiking. The main resort, towards the upper end of the valley at about 1,380m (4,525ft), is **Sölden**, plentifully provided with facilities of all kinds; skiing is possible well into summer. Above Zwieslstein the valley divides. To the southwest, directly

Ötzi

On 19 September 1991 a couple hiking in the Ötztaler Alps reported their discovery of a body in the ice on the border between Austria and Italy. The corpse turned out to be not the victim of a recent climbing accident, but a 5,300-year-old Celt. Instantly nicknamed 'Ötzi', the astonishingly well-preserved mountain man seems to have been killed by a flint arrowhead shot at him by unknown adversaries. Was he Austrian or Italian? The question threatened to destabilise the good relations between the two countries, but goodwill prevailed; after being thoroughly examined in Innsbruck, Ötzi was ceremoniously conveyed to a newly built museum in Bozen/Bolzano in South Tyrol, where he and the many belongings he had with him at the moment of his death can be admired today.

beneath the 3,774m (12,382ft) Wildspitze, the valley of the Ventner Ache leads to little **Vent**, a community boasting the highest permanently inhabited farm buildings in Tyrol. From here a trail climbs through the snowfields to the pass over the main ridge, close to the spot where famous Ötzi, the 'man in the ice', was found in 1991. To the east, the road through the Gurgler Tal climbs south to the popular winter sports village of **Obergurgl** at 1,920m (6,300ft), then beyond and even higher to **Hochgurgl**, before crossing the frontier at Timmelsjoch and dropping down steeply into South Tyrol.

To the west of the Ötztal, two other valleys lead from the Inn into the white world of the Ötztaler Alps. The **Pitztal** ends at Mittelberg in the shadow of the mighty Wildspitze. From here, the Pitzexpress funicular, then the Pitzpanorama-bahn take visitors to the foot of the Pitztal glacier, the highest point in Austria accessible by cable car (2,860m/9,383ft). Further west, beyond the town of Landeck, the **Kaunertal** also ends in a glacier. The well-engineered toll road known as the Kaunertaler Gletscher-Panoramastrasse climbs through forests and past the extensive Gepatsch reservoir before terminating by the glacier at a height of 2,750m (9,022ft).

Home of skiing

The Arlberg is one of the birthplaces of skiing, with the Arlberg Ski Club founded as long ago as 1901. In 1921 the first ski school was established by local man Hannes Schneider, and in 1928, together with the British winter sports pioneer Arnold Lunn, he inaugurated the classic downhill race for the Kandahar Cup.

The Arlberg

For centuries, the formidable massif of the **Arlberg** hindered communication between Tyrol and Austria's westernmost province, Vorarlberg. The perilous winter crossing of the Arlberg Pass (1,795m/5,885ft) claimed

Pristine slopes

many victims, though many others found refuge in the hospice maintained by the Brotherhood of St Christoph dating from 1386. A 10km (6-mile) -long rail tunnel was driven through the mountain in 1884, followed eventually by the 14km (9-mile) road tunnel opened in 1978. The Tyrolean gateway to the Arlberg is the small industrial town of **Landeck**, which stands at the meeting point of important road routes. From here the road through the upper valley of the Inn climbs southwestwards towards Italy and the Engadine in Switzerland, passing a number of low-key resort villages as well as a side road leading up to **Samnaun**. This anomaly of a village belongs to Switzerland but is only accessible from Austria. As well as being a minor ski resort, it also earns its living as a duty-free paradise. Further west, the road along the **Paznauntal** passes the popular ski resorts of **Ischgl** and **Galtür** on its way to the **Silvretta-Hochalpenstrasse** (see page 125), an alternative, high-altitude route into Vorarlberg.

The superb conditions have always attracted serious sportspeople, along with the rich, royal and famous, and the glamorous resort of **St Anton am Arlberg** has every right to revel in its reputation as a prestigious playground, where après-ski facilities match those on the slopes. Equally chic, but far smaller, is **St Christoph am Arlberg**, while the major resorts of **Zürs** and **Lech** are just over the border in Vorarlberg (see page 124).

VORARLBERG

With its head in the Alps, Austria's smallest and western-most province dips its toes into the broad waters of **Lake Constance** ㉘ ('Bodensee' in German), which it shares with Switzerland and Bavaria. The lake is a huge asset, the existence of international borders forming no barrier to visitors' enjoyment of the innumerable attractions along the shorelines of the three countries. The provincial capital, Bregenz, is an important gateway for visitors to Austria as a whole, as well as a fascinating destination in its own right. Inland, there is much to see and do, particularly in the rustic Bregenzerwald uplands and in the superlative

A brook in Vorarlberg

winter sports region of the
Arlberg, shared with Tyrol.
Vorarlberg is much closer to
Zürich than to Vienna, and
although it came into the
possession of the Habsburgs
in the 14th century, the barrier of the Arlberg inhibited
communication with the
rest of the country for centuries. Architecture, dialect
and folk customs reveal
how much the province has
in common with its Swiss
neighbour, which it made
an unsuccessful attempt to
join in the chaotic aftermath of World War I.

The Seebühne

Seated in tiers on the
landward side, some 7,000
spectators can enjoy the
operatic action taking place
on the floating stage of the
Bregenz Seebühne. The
repertoire consists of lavishly staged performances
of popular classics such as
Verdi's *Trovatore* or Puc-
cini's *Tosca*. Designers aim
to stun the public with the
boldness and originality
of their sets, which take
months to prepare.

Bregenz

With a population of less than 30,000, the little capital of
Vorarlberg exudes an importance out of all proportion to its
modest size. The town's enviable lakeside location beneath
Mount Pfänder, the splendidly landscaped waterside promenade and the bustling modern centre complemented by the
ancient upper town all combine to make it clear that this is
somewhere unique. Only made the official capital in 1918,
Bregenz has been most successful in promoting itself, notably with the **Bregenzer Festspiele**, one of Austria's most
ambitious festivals, an annual summertime jamboree of opera,
concerts and drama.

Separated from the town by the railway, and largely traffic-free, the promenade stretches along the shore of Lake
Constance, giving access to lake steamers, marinas, swimming
pools, and, above all, to the imposing group of structures

The pretty town of Bregenz

housing the casino, the festival and congress building, and the famous **Seebühne** or lake stage.

Much of the town centre is built on land reclaimed from the lake, whose original shoreline is marked by the late 17th-century **Seekapelle** (Lake Chapel). Nearby is the **Vorarlberger Landesmuseum** (Provincial Museum; Tue–Sun 9am–noon, 2–5pm; charge), with fascinating collections evoking the town's long history as well as a selection of works by Angelika Kauffmann (1741–1807), the painter from a Bregenzerwald family who achieved her greatest fame in London. Contemporary artworks are on show in the changing exhibitions staged by the **Kunsthaus Bregenz** (Tue–Sun 10am–6pm; charge), an uncompromising rectangle of concrete and etched glass designed by the celebrated Swiss architect Peter Zumthor.

A cobbled ramp climbs to the gateway guarding the **Oberstadt**, the charming Upper Town of tranquil lanes and little squares. This was the original core of Bregenz, occupied successively by Bronze Age folk, Celts, Romans, Alemannic tribespeople and the medieval counts of Bregenz. The main landmark is the **Martinsturm**, a medieval tower topped by a bulbous onion dome.

The favourite short trip from Bregenz is by cable car to the summit of Mount **Pfänder** (1,064m/3,491ft), from where there are fine views over lake, Alps and the broad valley of the Rhine.

The Bregenzerwald

No longer the vast forest its name might imply, this upland region was cleared of much of its woodland centuries ago, and is now characterised by glorious rolling pastureland rising to rocky peaks on the border with Bavaria and Tyrol. Before the building of a railway and good roads in the early 20th century, the rather remote Bregenzerwald was the home of independent-minded peasants, scornful, like their Swiss counterparts on the far side of the Rhine, of rule by feudal overlords. They were famed for their building skills, evident today in the area's heritage of fine old farmhouses clad in tiny wooden shingles, and they are still famous for their tasty, individually produced cheeses. Bypassed by today's mass tourism, the Bregenzerwald nevertheless has much to offer visitors, not least in the hospitality dispensed by an exceptional number of gourmet restaurants. There is superlative summer walking, and while winter sports may lack the glitz of the Arlberg resorts,

House in the Bregenzerwald

Local history museum in Schwarzenberg

there are plenty of slopes for all but the most adventurous skiers as well as a wonderfully cosy après-ski ambience in the many delightful villages. The main axis of the area is the Bregenzer Ache river, popular with wildwater enthusiasts. The course of the river is followed in part by the main road, which eventually climbs over the Hochtannenberg Pass (1,675m/5,495ft) then down to the little town of Warth and to the prestigious Arlberg winter resorts of **Lech** and **Zürs**. This is a highly scenic alternative to the direct route between Vorarlberg and Tyrol through the Arlberg Tunnel. Time should be allowed to take side roads to attractive villages such as **Bezau** or **Damüls** or to the native place of the Kauffmann family, **Schwarzenberg**, which boasts a particularly fine grouping of traditional buildings and a church decorated by their most famous offspring, Angelika.

Feldkirch and the Montafon

To the south of Bregenz, main road, motorway and railway run parallel to the Rhine and the Swiss border through a busy landscape of farmland interrupted by a succession of towns and villages once based on textile manufacturing. **Dornbirn** is the largest settlement, **Feldkirch** the most interesting. Right on the border with the Principality of Liechtenstein, Feldkirch was mentioned as early as 842, though it only attained town status around 1200, when its grid of streets was laid out in the shadow of the Schattenburg, the castle built by Hugo of Montfort. Arcaded squares, gateways and the remnants of town walls lend it a special atmosphere, and its Gothic cathedral has a great treasure in the shape of a Descent from the Cross painted by the local artist Wolf Huber in 1521.

From Feldkirch, the main routes run southeast up the valley of the River Ill to the town of **Bludenz**, where they turn east towards the road and rail tunnels through the Arlberg and into Tyrol. The valley of the Ill continues upstream into the **Montafon**, a district of pretty resort villages with high mountains to either side. This is the gateway to the **Silvretta-Hochalpenstrasse** ㉙, a spectacularly scenic toll road that was built originally to service the construction of dams and hydroelectric installations, but now carries tourists high into the heart of the Silvretta range, then down into the Paznaun in Tyrol. From the **Bielehöhe** saddle (2031m/6664ft) there are stunning views across the vast Silvretta reservoir towards the snowy peak of Piz Buin (3,312m/10,867ft) on the frontier with Switzerland.

Feldkirch's beautiful setting

WHAT TO DO

For those drawn to the great outdoors, Austria is a paradise in both summer and winter, while millions more are attracted by its glorious heritage of art and architecture and its vibrant cultural life.

ACTIVE PURSUITS

Winter Sports

Most Austrians seem to have been born with their feet attached to skis or a snowboard; not surprising since with its reliable snowfall and mountainous terrain, their country is ideal for all forms of winter recreation. This, together with a tradition of hospitality and a well-developed infrastructure, has long attracted foreign visitors to its slopes in large numbers. Resorts like Lech, St Anton, Kitzbühel and Schladming are internationally famous and need little introduction, but there are countless others catering for all levels of proficiency.

Downhill skiing and snowboarding retain their supremacy, while cross-country skiing is increasingly recognised as a great all-round exercise, as is Nordic walking on the many prepared winter paths. Activity is concentrated in the Alps, but people take to skis whenever and wherever snow falls: in the uplands along the Czech border and even in the hilly outskirts of Vienna. Novices can easily tap into local expertise; most resorts offer instruction, almost invariably from friendly English speakers, as well as hire of all the necessary equipment. Après-ski is more developed in the larger resorts.

Other winter activities include tobogganing, bobsledding and curling. Skating on Austria's many frozen lakes is also

Enjoying the Austrian slopes

popular; the shallow Neusiedlersee sometimes becomes a huge ice sheet, crossed by ice yachts reaching speeds of 80kmh (50mph).

The season usually lasts from early December until early April, though all-year skiing can be practised at high altitudes, such as on the Dachstein, Tuxer and Stubai glaciers. The price of accommodation is at its highest over the Christmas and New Year period and in mid-February.

The Austrian Tourist Board publishes an annual guide to the country's winter sports regions and resorts.

Walking and Climbing

Few countries are as welcoming to the hiker as Austria. Its hills and mountains, lakes and rivers, meadows and forests are linked by a dense network of footpaths, with the higher ground made easily accessible by cable cars and chair-lifts.

Hiking in Zell am See

Ubiquitous mountain restaurants mean that day walkers hardly ever need to carry provisions, while longer, more challenging high-level tours are facilitated by the presence of hundreds of Alpine huts offering basic (and not-so-basic) overnight accommodation as well as meals. Such huts are owned and run by a variety of organisations, of which the most important is the Österreichischer Alpenverein (Austrian

Austria is a great place to ski

Alpine Club; www.alpenverein.at, in German) which has a British branch (www.aacuk.org.uk). Club membership brings numerous benefits including reduced rates for accommodation in the mountain huts.

Experienced walkers will find it possible to conquer many a peak without special equipment or a guide or needing to indulge in serious scrambling. Routes are usually well signposted, though not on any standardised national system. In Vorarlberg, the excellent Swiss model of waymarking has been introduced. Most localities offer various themed walks, and there are numerous long-distance trails such as the Tyrolean Adlerweg (Eagle Walk) which links St Johann in the east of the province with St Anton am Arlberg in the west.

Tourist information centres are good sources of information about local walks for all levels of ability and can sometimes supply useful free maps showing recommended routes. Excellent maps with footpaths clearly marked are published by the Austrian Alpine Club, Kompass and Freytag & Berndt.

The right gear

All walkers should bear in mind that weather conditions can change very rapidly in the Alps, and that a sunny morning is no guarantee of fine weather later in the day. A rainproof jacket or coat, a warm underlayer and stout footwear are not options, but essential equipment, even if the planned walk is just a ramble from the top station of a cable car.

Most maps are at a scale of 1:50,000, but where available, maps at 1:25,000 scale show a much greater degree of detail and are highly recommended.

Numerous travel agents offer walking holiday packages that free participants from the need to carry luggage from one overnight stop to the next. One route served in this way is the Dachstein Rundwanderweg (Dachstein Circle), an eight-day trail taking in some of the finest scenery of the Salzkammergut and including an ascent by cable car almost to the summit of the Dachstein itself. Further information is available from www.dachstein-rundwanderweg.at.

The Austrian Alps offer serious climbers and mountaineers endless possibilities, while novices can learn to tackle the bare rock at one of the many mountain climbing schools. Even the completely uninitiated can, if fit, sign up for adventurous experiences such as a guided tour of a glacier. The Austrian Alpine Club (www.alpenverein.at) can supply details of climbing schools, instructors and courses.

Cycling

Austria is one of Europe's most bike-friendly countries. Most towns have a network of cycle lanes and places to park a bike, while in the countryside there are thousands of kilometres of cycle tracks. It is easy to hire a bike, either from a bicycle shop or at the main railway stations, which offers the advantage that the rented two-wheeler can be left at another station after use.

Mountain biking has become ever more popular; the province of Salzburg, for example, has over 2,000km (1,240 miles) of marked mountain-bike trails. The course of many a river is followed by a cycle path: the favourite is probably the route along the Danube, which runs all the way from Passau in Bavaria to Vienna and on to Bratislava with hardly a climb to hinder progress, but there are many others as well as trails around the Wörthersee and other lakes. Details of trails and organised tours can be found on www.oesterreich-radreisen.at (in German) or in a useful brochure published by the Austrian National Tourist Office.

Cycling in an Alpine setting

Water Recreation

Austria more than makes up for its lack of a coastline with its wealth of other water resources – unpolluted rivers, mountain torrents and thousands of lakes, ranging from icy mountain tarns to the broad expanses of Carinthia's Wörthersee and Burgenland's Neusiedlersee, to say nothing of Vorarlberg's share of ocean-like Lake Constance. The water in many of the lakes in the Salzkammergut is drinkably pure.

All kinds of water activity are possible. The Neusiedlersee is a veritable paradise for yachtspeople, windsurfers and kitesurfers, while rafters and canyoners should head for the Rivers Enns and Steyr. Canoeists are also well provided for. The *Strandbad*, or lido, is a fixture on many a lakeshore, notably in Carinthia, where geographical conditions mean that lakes warm rapidly in summer, some reaching a temperatures of around 28°C (82.5°F).

The crystal-clear waters of many lakes lend themselves to diving: for example, in Carinthia's Weissensee, the Grundlsee in Styria, and in the Hallstätter See in the Salzkammergut, where there is a diving school. The Hallstättersee is also famous for its oversize pike, and here, as well as elsewhere in lakes and rivers, there are plenty of opportunities for anglers to get reeling.

Other Sports

As a top holiday destination, Austria makes sure its visitors are provided with sports facilities of all kinds. Tennis courts abound, while a relaxing round of golf can be enjoyed in picturesque settings in many areas. Horse riders have riding centres and 8,000km (500 miles) of bridle paths at their disposal. Hang-gliding and paragliding are extremely popular.

Austrians enjoy all the usual spectator sports, with ice hockey commanding a special following in some regions. Football was given a great boost in summer 2008, when the country, together with Switzerland, hosted the European Cup

Spas

Many visitors to Austria combine an active holiday with relaxation at one of the many spa resorts. 'Taking the waters' is done in style in Austria; the many natural sources have been supplemented by an array of ever more sophisticated treatments designed to cure or alleviate medical conditions, as well as offering straightforward pampering. Spa facilities are generally excellent, and are constantly being added to, with a range of accommodation to suit most budgets. The national tourist office publishes a useful brochure giving details of spas all over the country.

at stadiums in Innsbruck, Salzburg, Klagenfurt and Vienna.

SHOPPING

While Austria has its share of supermarkets, department stores, shopping malls and even the monster 'Shopping City Süd' at Vösendorf just outside Vienna, Austrians are discriminating consumers and appreciate small, specialist shops and regular open-air markets. The quality of food products is high, and organic produce is widely available. Packaging is kept to a minimum, as is the free handing out of plastic bags. Craft traditions are still strong, though

The many variations of the ubiquitous Mozartballs

this has not stopped the proliferation of souvenir shops and stalls offering tourists the most shameless kind of kitsch. The historic central streets and squares of many towns have either been closed to traffic or its impact has been minimised, making strolling and shopping a real pleasure. There are usually plenty of open-air cafés and other places in which to sit and recover from your spending spree while admiring your purchases.

Things to buy

Crafts. Some of the best souvenirs are sold in the *Heimatwerk* shops to be found in the centre of most provincial capitals. Specialising in the work of local craftspeople, they are

Lederhosen

neither cheap nor outrageously expensive and of good quality. The stock varies by region, but usually includes traditional clothing using loden and other materials, fabrics, china and glassware and timber articles. While *lederhosen* or a *dirndl* may look rather odd once you get them back home, there are usually updated versions of jackets, coats, shirts and blouses that can be worn anywhere.

Museum shops are always worth investigating for unusual items, while visitors to the Swarovski Kristallwelten exhibition will be tempted by the wide selection of crystal, glassware and jewellery on sale. Good reproductions of the design icons of the country's turn-of-the-century golden era can be found in shops like Woka in Vienna.

Food and drink. Austria's supreme culinary achievements are the cakes, tarts and pastries on sale in the *Konditorei*, of which the most famous examples are Demel and Gerstner in Vienna. Packaged sweeties include Salzburg's *Mozartkugeln* (chocolate-coated marzipan and nougat balls) and Zotter chocolates from Styria. Many delicatessens are true temples to gastronomy, none more so than the capital's Meinl am Graben in Kohlmarkt. Fresh foodstuffs and local specialities like Styria's delicious pumpkin-seed oil can be bought at the open-air markets in most towns; Vienna's famous Naschmarkt with its fabulous range of produce and places of refreshment is open daily, while Salzburg's Schrannenmarkt and those in other cities may only operate on certain days of the week.

Rarely exported, Austrian wines and spirits are generally of high quality and make excellent gifts.

ENTERTAINMENT

Austria is devoted to its musical and operatic heritage, one of the country's great attractions for visitors from abroad. A solid programme of year-round cultural activity is supplemented by a rich palette of festivals; many of them, like Salzburg's, are of international renown. Popular culture and entertainment is vibrant too, with folk traditions lovingly maintained and some sort of 'scene' in the larger towns.

Classical Music, Opera and Theatre

Traditional oom-pah music

Vienna remains unrivalled as a centre for classical music and opera, and continues to pay tribute to the extraordinary roll-call of composers associated with the city, among them Haydn, Mozart, Beethoven, Schubert, Brahms, Bruckner, Mahler, Schönberg and Webern. The **Staatsoper** is one of the world's top opera houses, as is its orchestra, the **Wiener Philharmoniker**, who otherwise perform in the **Musikverein**. Tickets for the Staatsoper are notoriously difficult to get, though inexpensive standing places are put on sale shortly before each performance. Opera and classical music can also be enjoyed in the capital at the **Volksoper** and the **Kammeroper**, in Graz at the **Grazer Oper** and in Linz at the **Brucknerhaus**. In summer, an evocative spot in which to succumb to the charm of the waltz is by the statue of Strauss the Younger in Vienna's Stadtpark. For anyone with a command of German, a visit to the capital's great **Burgtheater** is likely to prove an unforgettable experience. For others, the appeal of drama is obviously limited, though Vienna does have an **English Theatre**. Visitors should note that Austrians take high culture seriously and dress appropriately; in formal evening-wear, for example, when attending the opera.

Other Music

Austrian pop may have a dismal record of nul points in the Eurovision Song Contest, but rock and pop fans will always

Seeing an orchestra in Vienna is a must

find something to their liking in city clubs and bars, above all in the Naschmarkt and Spittelberg areas of Vienna. Visitors in search of local colour will enjoy sentimental *Schrammelmusik* in the *Heuriger* taverns of Vienna's wine villages or, in the country, the rousing sound of brass bands manned by burly bearded types in

Schrammelmusik

Viennese *Schrammelmusik* features violin, guitar and accordion, and is best enjoyed in the convivial setting of one of the city's wine taverns, where drinkers also soak up sentimental songs with titles such as *Wien, Wien, nur Du allein* ('Vienna, Vienna, just you alone').

loden jackets and white socks. The country has yet to suffer a shortage of expert yodellers, whose talents are deployed at every tourist resort in the land.

Cinema
As elsewhere, Hollywood dominates the screen, and many English-language films are shown in the original version (look for 'OV' in the listings). Others have subtitles in German ('OmU'), while films designated 'OmeU' are generally German-language films with English subtitles. Probably the most evocative film ever made with Vienna as its setting is *The Third Man*. There are regular showings of this film at Vienna's Burgkino in Mariahilferstrasse.

Festivals
The Roman Catholic Church continues to play a significant part in the life of the country, and the main religious festivals are important events in the annual calendar.

During Advent many towns have Christmas markets, with carol singing, brass bands and *Glühwein*. St Nicholas (Santa Claus) appears on 6 December to reward good children with gifts, but not before naughty ones have been chastised the evening before by a devil-like figure called Krampus. The feast of the Three Kings marks the end of the Christmas season, when children go from door to door hoping to be given sweets.

Easter sees prayers at Stations of the Cross and a vigil on the night before Easter Sunday. Homes and shops are decorated with pussy willow, and children hunt for decorated eggs. Corpus Christi is marked by processions in localities including Bischofshofen, Gmunden, Deutschlandsberg and in Hallstatt, where it takes place on the lake aboard flower-bedecked boats.

Folk festivals were regarded as superstitious nonsense by 18th-century Emperor Joseph II, who did his best to stamp them out. But some survive, notably the *Perchtenlauf* processions in Tyrol and Salzburger Land where the participants wear grotesque masks. Among the most popular celebrations are local *Schützenfeste*, where marksmen parade through the streets in traditional garb and take part in a shooting competition. In late September and early October the wine harvest is celebrated in Burgenland, Lower Austria and the wine districts of Styria. The most festive time of the year is *Fasching*, or Carnival, the revelry marking the beginning

Christmas market in Vienna

of Lent. Vienna's *Fasching* celebrations include some 300 balls, the most prestigious being the *Opernball* at the Staatsoper.

As befits this most musical of nations, hardly a month passes without some music festival, not just in Vienna and Salzburg but in more modest locations such as the Vorarlberg village of Schwarzenberg with its annual Schubert Festival in June.

CHILDREN'S AUSTRIA

Austria offers children's activities of all kinds. Kids can learn to climb, ski, go white-water rafting, practise traditional crafts in an open-air village museum, help feed the animals on a farm, pan for gold in a mountain stream, explore ice caves or hurtle down a timber chute in an old salt mine. Conventional attractions include zoos, puppet shows, and Klagenfurt's amazing Minimundus model city. As well as its world-famous ferris wheel, Vienna's Prater has a huge amusement park, and there is another one at the Swarovski Crystal World near Innsbruck. Even getting around the country can be fun, especially aboard a river steamer, a narrow-gauge steam train or high above the ground on a chair-lift. The Zoom Kindermuseum in Vienna is devoted to children, from infants upwards.

Other facilities for children are normally of a high standard. Most towns have good playgrounds, and restaurants usually have a kid's menu and highchairs. Many hotels offer baby-sitting, while others, grouped together as *Kinderhotels*, www.kinderhotels.co.uk, offer families a comprehensive service, including free childcare, baby and toddler equipment and a full range of services and activities. The ultimate in this kind of provision is the Baby-und-Kinderdorf in Trebesing, www.babydorf.at (in German), a Carinthian mountain village with a range of accommodation and enough activities to keep guests amused from dawn to dusk.

Calendar of Events

January Boisterous parties begin on New Year's Eve (called *Silvester*) and the *Kaiserball* opens the ball season in Vienna's Hofburg. At midnight, the chimes of Vienna's St Stephan's Cathedral are broadcast. New Year's Day concert by the Vienna Philharmonic Orchestra. Mozart Week music festival in Salzburg.

March/April Bregenz Spring festival of classical music.

Easter Salzburg Easter music festival.

Vienna *Osterklang* (Sounds of Easter) music festival.

May *Gauderfest* beer festival in Zell im Zillertal.

May/June *Wiener Festwochen* (Vienna Festival Weeks) featuring music, dance, drama and film.

June/July Lower Austria Danube festival of all the arts, various locations. Innsbruck *Tanzsommer* festival of dance.

July Graz *Styriarte* classical music festival.

July–August Salzburg International Festival of opera, music and drama. Bregenz Festival of music and opera with performances on a floating stage on Lake Constance.

Innsbruck Festival of Ancient Music in Schloss Ambras.

Jazzfest Wien with concerts in the Staatsoper and Burgtheater.

Vienna *Klangbogen* music recitals in palaces and outdoor locations and Vienna *Musiksommer* of opera and operetta.

Mörbisch Lakeside Festival of operetta on the Neusiedlersee.

Bad Ischl festival of operetta.

August/September Spittal an der Drau drama festival in the courtyard of Schloss Porcia.

September Haydn Festival in Schloss Esterhazy in Eisenstadt.

September/October Linz International Bruckner festival.

October Graz Styrian Autumn avant-garde festival of all the arts.

Vienna *Viennale* film festival and *Wien Modern* festival of contemporary classical music.

Zell am Ziller *Alpabtrieb* celebrations to mark the return of cattle from the Alpine pastures.

EATING OUT

No visitor to Austria is likely to go hungry in a country whose traditional cuisine is hearty, filling and provided in lavish quantities. At the centre of a great empire, the local diet has always been affected by influences from other cuisines, though Austrian cooks tended to modify Italian, Czech or Hungarian recipes to suit themselves. What is perhaps the most famous of all Austrian dishes, the *Wiener Schnitzel*, has its origins in Italy's *costoletto alla milanese*, while the beef stew going under the name of *gulasch* bears little resemblance to its fiery Hungarian counterpart. Nowadays, although the influences are global ones and there are plenty of establishments specialising in exotic cuisines, the typical restaurant meal will still have a distinctly Austrian character.

Traditional *Wiener Schnitzel*

WHEN TO EAT

Breakfast (Frühstück). At home, this is quite likely to be the simplest of meals, perhaps just a cup of coffee or tea and a bread roll or two. But most hotels of any standing serve their guests with a cornucopia of cereals, eggs, sausages and cooked meats, cheeses, yoghurts, different

Snacks

The most popular snack is a *Wurst* (sausage), bought from a stall in the street and consumed on the spot. Sausages come in various shapes and sizes, the most common being frankfurters, known as *Wiener* (Viennese) except in Vienna where they are called *Würstel*.

kinds of bread and cakes, all washed down with fruit juice, tea and coffee.

Lunch (Mittagessen). For many Austrians, this is the main meal of the day, starting with soup, going on to a meat- or fish-based main course with vegetables and potatoes or dumplings, and ending with a delicious, calorie-rich dessert. Restaurants normally offer a *Mittagsmenu* or *Tagesmenu* – an inexpensive set meal, usually of two courses and by no means of inferior quality to the dishes described in the *Speisekarte*, the à la carte menu. Lunch is usually eaten quite early.

Dinner (Abendessen or Nachtmahl). If eaten at home, this meal is likely to be a relatively modest affair of soup, cold cuts, salad and bread, while restaurants may offer an expanded version of the midday menu.

WHAT TO EAT

Backhendl. Fried chicken, prepared like *Wienerschnitzel* in a coating of egg and breadcrumbs.

Bauernschmaus. 'Farmer's Feast', a plateful of sausage, bacon, chunks of meat, potatoes or dumplings and sauerkraut.

Beuschel. A creamy ragout made from lights (lungs) and heart of veal or pork, usually served with a bread dumpling and probably more appreciated by locals than by visitors.

Brot. Austrian bread is among the best in the world, and comes in a variety of forms, from a delicate white *Semmel* (roll) to a big brown loaf, crisp on the outside, deliciously moist and tasty on the inside.

Fisch. While ocean fish are available, river and lake fish are much more common and should be tried. *Forelle* (trout) is perhaps the most familiar, at its tastiest when served *au bleu* or *Müllerin* (crisply sautéed in butter). *Fogosch* or *Zander* (pike-perch) is a Hungarian speciality, but much appreciated in Austria too. *Karpfen* (carp) traditionally graces the table on Christmas Eve and at New Year.

Gefüllte Paprika. Peppers stuffed with meat and rice.

Gulasch. Usually made with beef and spicy enough for most tastes, a thick *Gulaschsuppe* (goulash soup) can be a meal in itself. *Fiakergulasch* (Cabby's goulash) is topped with a fried egg, *Szegediner Gulasch* has sauerkraut and cream mixed in.

Knödel. Dumplings are made from flour, crumbled white rolls or potato, and are ideal for soaking up rich sauces.

Schweinsbraten. Pork joint roasted with carrot, celery, onion, garlic and potatoes.

Alfresco in Innsbruck

Apple strudel and coffee – an Austrian speciality

Suppe. Soup is one of the staples of the Austrian table. The commonest is *Rindsuppe* (beef broth), which forms the basis of many a concoction, such as *Leberknödelsuppe*, broth with delicate liver dumplings floating in it.

Tafelspitz. Reputedly Emperor Franz Joseph's favourite, this is perhaps the most celebrated of all Austrian meat dishes, consisting of a lean cut of beef boiled and served with a chive sauce, spinach, horseradish and apple purée.

Wiener Schnitzel. Tender cut of veal (sometimes pork), dipped in flour, egg and breadcrumbs, fried, garnished with lemon and served with potato or cucumber salad.

Provincial Specialities

Burgenland. On the edge of the Hungarian *puszta*, this is the place to sample food with a Magyar touch, such as roast goose, and even better *Gänseleber*, roast goose liver with onions.

Carinthia. The local version of ravioli, *Käsnudeln*, are delicious filled with curd cheese and mint, or even with fruit. The province is also rich in *Wild* (game).

Lower Austria. The Marchfeld district to the east of Vienna supplies the capital with succulent *Spargel* (asparagus), while the Wachau produces not only wine but quantities of *Marillen* (apricots), often served as a dessert encased in a dumpling and sprinkled with dry cottage cheese.

Salzburg. Apart from *Mozartkugeln*, the city is famous for the mouth-watering soufflé known as *Salzburger Nockerl*.

Styria. The province's pumpkin harvest yields seeds which are ground, roasted and pressed to make *Kürbiskernöl*, a nutty-flavoured dark green oil which gives a special edge to salads, soups, main dishes and even desserts.

Tyrol. *Bauernspeck* (farm-cured bacon) is used in the province's tasty dumplings as well as eaten on its own.

Upper Austria. The area's best-known speciality is *Linzer Torte*, a layer cake covered with latticed strips of dough.

Vorarlberg. The cheese from the pastures of the Bregenzerwald gives *Kässpätzle* noodles their flavour.

Desserts

Sinfully sweet desserts *(Mehlspeisen)* are one of Austria's greatest contributions to the international food scene. As well as those mentioned above, there are *Buchteln*, yeast buns filled with *Powidl* (concentrated plum jam); doughnut-like *Krapfen*; *Palatschinken* (pancakes stuffed with jam, curd cheese or nuts); and of course *Apfelstrudel*. Apples are the traditional filling of a *Strudel*, but other possibilities include fruit such as damsons and sweet or sour cherries, poppy seeds and ground walnuts. A *Topfenstrudel* is made from curd cheese, while a *Rahmstrudel* is filled with cream. The essence of a *Strudel* is its pastry, which should be transparent enough to read a newspaper through it. Of all the *Torten*

Socialising over a drink in Vienna

tempting the passer-by from the windows of the *Konditorei*, the most appetising has to be the *Sachertorte*. Invented in 1832 to please the jaded palate of Prince Metternich, this confection of dark chocolate cake and apricot jam has ruled supreme ever since. Its name is legally protected, in that Vienna's Hotel Sacher has the sole right to call it *Sachertorte*; all competitors must be content with *Sacher Torte*.

WHAT TO DRINK

Wine

Wine is one of Austria's best-kept secrets. Austrians are keen wine drinkers, and this, coupled with the fact that barely enough is produced locally to satisfy their demands, means that little wine is exported and known abroad. Whatever international reputation Austrian wine once had was ruined by the great glycol scandal of 1985, when a tiny minority of producers were found to be giving their wine extra 'body' by adulterating it with antifreeze. A shocked industry reacted by introducing one of the world's strictest regulatory regimes, and the Austrian wines of today are some of the purest and finest in the world. No meal is wholly satisfying without at least a *Viertel* (0.25l measure) to complement it, and no trip to the country's wine-growing areas is complete without sampling the wares of a *Heuriger* or *Buschenschank*, a rustic tavern serving the vintner's fresh produce straight from the barrel. Touring motorists will enjoy following well-signposted *Weinstrassen* (Wine Roads) through the vineyards.

The country's wine-producing regions are nearly all in the lower-lying, sunny east and southeast. The most extensive area is in Lower Austria, in the Weinviertel (Wine District) and along the Danube, where the gorge-like Wachau forms one of Europe's classically picturesque wine regions. Apart from Riesling, the most important grape variety here is Austria's signature grape, Grüner Veltliner; both make very palatable white wines. Reds as well as whites come from that part of the Weinviertel

Das Kaffeehaus

Austria generally, and Vienna in particular, can be said to have given the world the archetypal Central European coffee house: cathedrals of caffeine where, for the price of a single cup, time could traditionally be spent reading the newspaper, engaging in intellectual conversation or writing a novel. *Kaffeehäuser* still thrive, offering a bewildering range of up to 30 options: a *Schwarzer* or *Mocca* is a straightforward small black coffee, a *Verlängerter* a longer, diluted version; a *Brauner* has a dash of milk; while a *Melange* is like a cappuccino and an *Einspänner* is one of many coffees enhanced by the addition of whipped cream.

Spirits

Austria produces an array of palatable fruit brandies, ranging from *Himbeergeist* (raspberry) to *Marillenschnapps* (apricot) and *Sliwowitz* (plum), all of them a good way of rounding off a satisfying meal.

running parallel to the border with Slovakia, where many villages have whole streets of little wine cellars built into the hillside. Vienna is the world's only capital where vineyards flourish in the city itself, tumbling down from the hills of the Vienna Woods into suburban villages like Grinzing and Nussdorf. Downstream from Vienna there are further vineyards, and more still in Burgenland around Neusiedlersee, producing fine sweet wines. After the Wachau, the prettiest vineyards are those of southern Styria along the border with Slovenia, where the hilly landscape of vine-clad slopes and farmsteads has earned the name of 'Styrian Tuscany'. Here Sauvignon Blanc and Chardonnay predominate.

A wine label is likely to include information on the region, vineyard, grower and classification: a *Tafelwein* is a basic table wine, while a *Landwein* must come from a specific area; a *Qualitätswein* is of superior quality, a *Kabinett* even more so.

Beer

With a consumption per head third only to the Czech Republic and Germany, Austria can be said to have a well-developed beer culture. The favourite is lager-type beer, called here *Märzen*, normally quaffed from a 0.3l (*ein kleines Bier*) or 0.5l glass (*ein grosses Bier*). There are more than 150 breweries in total; popular brews include *Stiegel* from Salzburg, Styrian *Gösser*, and Vienna's *Ottakringer*. Real Pilsner from Pilsen in the Czech Republic is widely available on draught.

TO HELP YOU ORDER...

Waiter, waitress, please!	**Bedienung, bitte!**
Could we have a table?	**Wir hätten gerne einen Tisch.**
May I see the menu, please?	**Darf ich die Speisekarte sehen, bitte?**
The bill please.	**Zahlen bitte.**
I would like...	**Ich möchte gerne...**

Beer	**ein Bier**	Menu	**Speisekarte**
Bread	**Brot**	Milk	**Milch**
Butter	**Butter**	Mineral water	**Mineralwasser**
Cheese	**Käse**	Potatoes	**Erdäpfel**
Dessert	**Nachtisch**	Salad	**Salat**
Fish	**Fisch**	Soup	**Suppe**
Fruit	**Obst**	Sugar	**Zucker**
Fruit juice	**Fruchtsaft**	Tea	**Tee**
Ice cream	**Eis**	Wine	**Wein**
Meat	**Fleisch**		

...AND READ THE MENU

Auflauf	casserole	**Krebs**	crayfish
Debreziner	spicy sausage	**Kren**	horseradish
Ei/Eier	egg(s)	**Kuchen**	cake
Ente	duck	**Lamm**	lamb
Erdbeeren	strawberries	**Leber**	liver
Faschiertes	minced meat	**Nockerln**	dumplings
Fisolen	green beans	**Paradieser**	tomatoes
Guglhupf	coffee cake	**Rahm**	cream
Gurke	gherkin	**Rindfleisch**	beef
Kaiser-fleisch	cured pork spare ribs	**Rostbraten**	pot roast
Kaiser schmarrn	pancake with fruit compote	**Rotkraut**	red cabbage
		Schinken	ham
Kalb	veal	**Schweine-fleisch**	pork
Kirschen	cherries	**Zwiebeln**	onions

PLACES TO EAT

Restaurants are listed alphabetically and include a small number of the cafés for which Austria is famous. Price categories for restaurants are based on the cost, per person, of a dinner comprising starter, mid-priced main course and dessert (not including wine, coffee or service), and are indicated as follows:

€€€ over 40 euros   **€€** 20–40 euros
€ 20 euros and under

VIENNA

Demel € *Kohlmarkt 14, tel: 535 17 17.* A national institution and one-time supplier of sugary specialities to the Habsburg court, this splendid café and patisserie is world-renowned for the virtuoso presentation of its irresistible delicacies. 9am–7pm.

Entler €€€ *Schlusselgasse 2, tel: 504 35 85.* A little out of the immediate city centre, not far from the Taubstummengasse metro station, this highly recommended restaurant combines contemporary and traditional decor to set the perfect scene for some of the capital's best Austrian cuisine. Service is top-notch but be prepared to wait a little for your food as everything is prepared fresh.

Figlmüller €€ *Bäckerstrasse 6, tel: 512 17 60.* This is a branch of a long-established restaurant (at Wollzeile 5) popular with both locals and visitors for its Austrian favourites, notably plate-sized Wiener Schnitzels.

Gulaschmuseum € *Schulerstrasse 20, tel: 512 10 17.* Goulash is as popular in Austria as in its native Hungary. At the 'Goulash Museum' you can choose from a whole range of exceedingly tasty meat dishes, though there are also vegetarian versions.

Heuriger Reinprecht € *Grinzing, Cobenzlgasse 22, tel: 32 01 47 10.* This cheerful establishment opposite the parish church in the suburban wine village of Grinzing has everything a *Heuriger* wine tavern should, including vaulted interiors, a terraced garden, excellent wines, a large and varied buffet, and *Schrammelmusik* in the background. Closed weekdays Jan and Feb.

Korso bei der Oper €€€ *Mahlerstrasse 2, tel: 51 51 65 46.* As its name implies, this glittering restaurant in the prestigious Hotel Bristol is located right by the Opera, whose star performers are among its most enthusiastic patrons. The trend-setting cuisine, interpreting Austrian gastronomic traditions with great panache, has garnered numerous awards.

Österreicher im MAK €€ *Stubenring 5, tel: 714 01 21.* The café/restaurant of the Museum of Applied Arts (MAK) is a cut above most such institutions. A triumph of contemporary design in its own right, and under the direction of acclaimed chef Helmut Österreicher, it offers 21st-century takes on the classical Austrian repertoire, both inside and on its summer terrace.

Plachutta €€ *Wollzeile 38, tel: 512 15 77.* The author of a definitive book on traditional Austrian cooking, Ewald Plachutta presides over a number of establishments, including this busy city centre temple devoted to the worship of that most characteristic Viennese dish, *Tafelspitz*. The delicious boiled beef creation is available here in a tempting variety of versions.

Steirereck €€€ *Am Heumarkt 2 (Stadtpark), tel: 713 31 68.* Housed in a lovely building overlooking the River Wien in the middle of the Stadtpark, this is one of the city's top restaurants, serving creative versions of traditional Austrian cuisine in an atmospheric setting. Open for lunch and dinner. The basement *Meierei* (dairy) keeps longer hours, and is great for breakfasts, patisseries, inexpensive lunches and a fabulous array of cheeses.

Wrenkh €€ *Bauernmarkt 10, tel: 533 15 26.* As well as creating gourmet vegetarian meals, award-winning chef Christian Wrenkh passes on his knowledge and enthusiasm in participatory workshops designed to make cooking a pleasure. His restaurant also serves meat and fish dishes of an equally high standard. Closed Sun.

LOWER AUSTRIA

Jamek €€ *A-3610 Weissenkirchen in der Wachau, tel: 02715 22 35.* On the bank of the Danube in the heart of the Wachau vineyards, the Jamek estate produces some of the area's most distinguished wines. These can be sampled in the course of a tasting or savoured as the accompaniment to a gourmet meal. Mon–Thur for lunch, Fri for lunch and dinner.

Jell €€ *A-3500 Krems an der Donau, Hoher Markt 8, tel: 02732 823 45.* This cheery *Gasthaus* with its panelled rooms and attractive garden could be described as the Austrian equivalent of a gastropub. Ulli, the enthusiastic landlady, constantly improves on classic local specialities, served in liberal portions. Closed Mon, lunch only Sat–Sun.

Landhaus Bacher €€€ *A-3512 Mautern, Südtiroler Platz 2, tel: 02732 829 37.* On the far bank of the Danube opposite Krems, the chef at this extremely refined country restaurant has been repeatedly crowned with gastronomic awards. Her thoughtful interpretation of the best of Austrian and Mediterranean cuisine is complemented by fine wines from her husband's cellar. Closed Mon–Tue and Jan–Feb.

Loibnerhof €€ *A-3601 Dürnstein, Unterloiben 7, tel: 02732 828 90.* In the little settlement of Unterloiben, just east of Richard Lionheart's Dürnstein, this 400-year-old family establishment oozes charm as well as providing excellent locally flavoured food. Dine inside beneath cool vaults or relax outside among the ancient trees of an old orchard. Wines from the family vineyard. Closed Mon–Tue.

BURGENLAND

Haydnbräu € *A-7000 Eisenstadt, Pfarrgasse 22, tel: 02682 639 45.* As well as brewing its own beer, this establishment in the centre of the little capital of Burgenland provides good solid Austrian pub fare at very reasonable prices. There is a summer garden for fine weather.

Kloster am Spitz €€ *A-7083 Purbach am Neusiedlersee, Wald-siedlung 2, tel: 02683 55 19.* Housing guest rooms as well as an excellent restaurant, the buildings of this former monastery stand among vineyards bordering the Neusiedlersee. Regional specialities include Hungarian fish soup made from the occupants of the great lake, accompanied by the establishment's own wines. Wed evening–Sun.

Wirtshaus im Hofgassl €€ *A-7071 Rust am See, Rathausplatz 10, tel: 02685 607 63.* In the middle of Rust, historic vaulted stables have been turned into an award-winning restaurant, where local specialities are given a light, contemporary treatment. Fresh ingredients are guaranteed, with herbs from the establishment's own garden, and expert advice is at hand to help you choose among the many local wines on offer.

Zur Dankbarkeit €€ *A-7141 Podersdorf am See, Hauptstrasse 39, tel: 02177 22 23.* Family-run, this charming old country inn complete with garden offers unpretentious versions of regional cuisine accompanied by local wines. Apr–Nov Fri–Tue, Dec–Mar Fri–Sun.

STYRIA

An der Lage – Jaglhof €€ *A-8462 Gamlitz, Sernau 25, tel: 03454 66 75.* High up among the vine-clad hills of the famed 'Styrian Tuscany' landscape, this combined hotel-vinotheque-restaurant commands fabulous views and is an excellent place to get accustomed with the region's characteristic food and drink. Closed Tue and Wed.

Eckstein €€ *A-8010 Graz, Mehlplatz 3, tel: 0316 82 87 01.* A buzzing contemporary restaurant in the heart of Graz's Altstadt, just the place to sit outside and enjoy the city's ambience. The seasonal menu rings the changes on international dishes, giving them a touch of Styrian character.

Gasthof-Restaurant Fink €€ *A-8333 Riegersburg, Riegersburg 29, tel: 03153 8216.* This friendly family-run *Gasthof* has an attractive restaurant and a terrace offering views almost as good as those from mighty Riegersburg Castle itself. Closed Thur Nov–Apr.

Landhaus Keller €€ *A-8010 Graz, Schmiedgasse 9, tel: 0316 83 02 76.* Some of the province's best food is served in this ancient and atmospheric establishment next door to the Landhaus and Zeughaus in Graz. Summer courtyard. Booking advisable.

Thomawirt €€ *A-8010 Graz, Leonhardstraße 40–42, tel: 0316 32 86 37.* Located to the east of the city centre, the hearty menu at this popular dining spot includes lots of vegetarian fare, steaks and many other dishes with just a hint of the Mediterranean about them.

CARINTHIA AND EAST TYROL

Dolce Vita €€–€€€ *A-9020 Klagenfurt, Heuplatz 2, tel: 0463 554 99.* Hailed as Klagenfurt's best restaurant, this small and welcoming establishment provides the very best of Italian food; above all, fresh, delicious fish. The set lunches are a bargain, evening meals more expensive. Best to book. Closed Sat–Sun.

Gasthof Jerolitsch € *A-9201 Krumpendorf, Jerolitschstrasse 43, tel: 04229 23 79.* Welcoming *Gasthof* specialising in fish dishes, the ingredients of which may have been swimming not too long ago in the nearby Wörthersee.

Gasthaus im Landhaushof € *A-9020 Klagenfurt, Landhaushof 1, tel: 50 23 63.* Solid Austrian specialities are served in the equally solid surroundings of the Landhaus, the ancient seat of the government in the provincial capital. Summer dining in the courtyard.

Kaufmann & Kaufmann €€ *A-9500 Villach, Dietrichsteingasse 5, tel: 04242 258 71.* Friendly service and a tempting range of local specialities are characteristic of this attractive restaurant in Carinthia's second city. Closed Sun–Mon.

Mettnitzer €€ *A-9800 Spittal an der Drau, Neuer Platz 17, tel: 04762 358 99.* This exuberant late 19th-century building in the middle of Spittal an der Drau has kept its original interiors; a fine place to tuck into substantial local dishes. Summer terrace. Closed Mon–Tue.

La Taverna €€ *A-9900 Lienz, Hauptplatz 14, tel: 04852 644 44 77.* Part of the prestigious Romantik Hotel Traube on the main square of Lienz, this cosy restaurant is known for its tempting Italian specialities. Closed Mon.

UPPER AUSTRIA

Gelbes Krokodil € *A-4020 Linz, OK Platz 1, tel: 070 78 41 82.* The urbane 'Yellow Crocodile' café-restaurant at the heart of the trendy Movimento arts cinema complex serves local and vegetarian food in a stylish setting. Daily; dinner only Sat–Sun.

Landhotel Mader €€ *A-4400 Steyr, Stadtplatz 36, tel: 07252 53 35 80.* On the glorious main square of historic Steyr, this long-established hotel caters for all tastes in a variety of different settings. There is the elegant 'Schubertstübl', a vaulted wine cellar, a cosy pub-type bar, and in summer a lovely arcaded courtyard or the square itself. The gourmet set meal is a great, and delicious, deal. Closed Sun.

Verdi €€€ *A-4040 Linz, Pachmayrstrasse 137, tel: 070 73 30 05.* High up above the city centre of Linz on the far bank of the Danube, this sophisticated restaurant is a favourite destination for city dwellers in search of fine dining. A second restaurant on the premises, Verdi Einkehr, is marginally less refined and offers more regionally based dishes. Tue–Sat for dinner.

SALZKAMMERGUT

Konditorei Zauner € *A-4820 Bad Ischl, Pfarrgasse 7, tel: 06132 23 31 013.* Founded in 1832 and possibly the most venerable establishment of its kind in Austria, this gorgeous patisserie and café once supplied the Imperial Court with delicious sugary delicacies during its summer retreat to Bad Ischl. Truly special. Daily 8.30am–6pm.

Post am See €€ *A-8993 Grundlsee, Bräuhof 94, tel: 03622 201 04.* In a fresh modern style, which nevertheless pays tribute to its glorious lake-and-mountain setting, this immaculately run restaurant extends right into Lake Grundlsee. Refined dishes include delicious local *Saibling* (char). May–Oct Wed–Sun.

Seegasthof Lackner €€ *A-5310 Mondsee, Mondseestrasse 1, tel: 06232 23 59.* Local dishes are given a light, international touch in this restaurant and served in appealing surroundings overlooking the water at the northern end of the Mondsee. Substantial vinotheque.

Villa Schratt €€ *A-4820 Bad Ischl, Steinbruch 43, tel: 06132 276 47.* The villa once lived in by Emperor Franz Joseph's 'dear friend', the actress Katherina Schratt, is now an attractive restaurant with a weekly changing menu. *Gugelhupf,* a tall ring of sponge cake ubiquitous across most of central Europe, is still baked here according to the elderly ruler's favourite recipe. Closed Tue–Wed.

SALZBURG AND SALZBURGER LAND

Bertahof €€ *A-5630 Bad Hofgastein, Vorderschneeberg 15, tel: 06432 76 08.* A warm welcome is guaranteed as long as you book your table in advance to eat at this rustic, 350-year-old chalet in a spa village in the Gastein valley. Specialities include home-raised lamb and fish from the restaurant's own pond. Fri–Sun only.

Bio-Wirtshaus Hirschenwirt €€ *A-5020 Salzburg, St-Julien-Strasse 23, tel: 0662 88 13 35.* The Hirschenwirt Hotel houses the city's only fully organic restaurant, serving tasty dishes at modest prices. Attractive garden for alfresco dining in summer. Closed Sun.

Café Tomaselli € *A-5020 Salzburg, Alter Markt 9, tel: 0662 84 44 88.* This traditional establishment had already been serving patrons for 50 years when owner Tomaselli was appointed 'Chocolatmacher' to the Archbishop's court in 1753. Order your *Melange* on one of the café's two floors or sit on the outdoor terrace and watch the Festival-goers. Mon–Sat 7am–9pm, Sun from 8am (until 10pm during Festival).

Carpe Diem Finest Fingerfood €€ *A-5020 Salzburg, Getreidegasse 50, tel: 0662 84 88 00.* Consisting of café, bar and restaurant, this innovative and stylish establishment on Salzburg's most famous street serves inventive and delicious 'fingerfood' in home-baked cones.

Die Weisse € *A-5020 Salzburg, Rupertgasse 10, tel: 0662 87 22 46.* On the right bank of the River Salzach, this big beer hall specialises in wheat beer and hearty traditional food at very reasonable prices. Closed Sun.

Esszimmer €€€ *A-5020 Salzburg, Müllner Hauptstrasse 33, tel: 0662 87 08 99.* Cutting-edge designer establishment with video screens and views into the kitchen. The food is refined Austrian with an international touch, best sampled at lunch time when relatively inexpensive dishes of the day are served. Evening reservations advisable. Closed Sun–Mon, except in Dec and during Festival.

Magazin €€€ *A-5020 Salzburg, Augustinergasse 13, tel: 0662 841 58 40.* At the foot of the Mönchsberg, much-praised Magazin has been described as a 'gastronomic conglomerate'. You can dine simply at the bar, deep underground in the 'Kaverne' let into the bare rock of the mountain, or with great refinement in the glazed gallery. The complex also has a vinotheque and a kitchen boutique. Evening reservations advisable. Closed Sun, except during Festival.

Mayer's, Schloss Prielau €€€ *A-5700 Zell am See, Hofmannsthalstrasse 12, tel: 06542 72 91 10.* Set in its very own park just to the north of Zell am See, this distinguished country house hotel has an elegant gourmet restaurant attached to it, where the prices are high, but more than justified. Booking is recommended to avoid disappointment. The hotel dining room also serves excellent, less expensive lunches. Closed Tue, dinner only Mon and Wed–Fri.

TYROL

Dengg €€ *A-6020 Innsbruck, Riesengasse 11–13, tel: 0512 58 23 47.* Housed in an ancient building in the heart of Innsbruck's Altstadt, this combined café, bar and restaurant offers up-to-date decor and inventive global cuisine. Closed Sat morning and Sun.

Ottoburg €€ *A-6020 Innsbruck, Herzog-Friedrichstrasse 1, tel: 0512 58 43 38.* An unmissable landmark on the riverbank at the edge of Innsbruck's Altstadt, 13th-century 'Otto's Castle' dishes up historic atmosphere as well as providing hearty Austrian fare. Closed Mon.

Ritter-Oswald-Stube €€€ *A-6100 Seefeld, Hotel Klosterbräu, Klosterstrasse 30, tel: 05212 262 11 00.* Gourmet restaurant in Seefeld's most prestigious hotel, offering Austrian and Mediterranean specialities in a refined Alpine setting. The basement Bräukeller focuses on traditional fare at less extravagant prices.

Wirtshaus Schöneck €€€ *A-6020 Innsbruck, Weiherburggasse 6, tel: 0512 27 27 28.* With fine views over Innsbruck's rooftops, this completely renovated establishment is one of the most acclaimed restaurants in town, well worth the slight detour for its excellent classical cuisine. Booking advisable. Hours vary.

VORARLBERG

Neubeck €€ *A-6900 Bregenz, Anton-Schneider-Strasse 5, tel: 05574 436 09.* This attractive establishment in the centre of Bregenz provides a range of refined French, Mediterranean and Asian dishes, which can be savoured in the Art Nouveau style interior, the winter garden or the inner courtyard. Good range of open wines. Closed Sun–Mon.

Romantikhotel Hirschen €€ *A-6867 Schwarzenberg, Hof 14, tel: 05512 29 44.* In the cosy panelled rooms of one of the prettiest buildings of this upland village, the Hirschen offers some of the best food in the Bregenzerwald, making it a popular destination for gourmets from the valley below. Thur eve–Tue.

A–Z TRAVEL TIPS

A Summary of Practical Information

A Accommodation . . . 160
Airports. 161
B Bicycle Hire. 162
Budgeting for
Your Trip 162
C Camping and
Caravanning 164
Car Hire 164
Climate 164
Clothing. 165
Crime and
Safety. 165
D Driving 165
E Electricity. 167
Embassies and
Consulates 167
Emergencies 168
G Gay and Lesbian
Travellers. 169
Getting There 169
Guides and Tours . . . 171

H Health and Medical
Care. 171
L Language 172
M Maps. 172
Media. 173
Money 173
O Opening Hours 174
P Police 174
Post Offices 175
Public Holidays. 175
T Telephone. 176
Time Zone 176
Tipping. 176
Toilets. 176
Tourist Information 177
Transport 177
V Visas and Entry
Requirements . . . 179
W Websites and Internet
Access 179
Y Youth Hostels. 180

A

ACCOMMODATION *(Unterkunft)* (see also Camping, Youth Hostels, and the list of Recommended Hotels on page 181)

As might be expected in a land with a long tradition of hospitality, Austria offers a friendly greeting, excellent service and a wide choice of places to stay. Hotels are regularly inspected and graded into five categories defined by numbers of stars. A five-star establishment will offer every service and great comfort, while the accommodation in a one-star hotel will be simple but almost certainly decent and well maintained, though possibly not with en suite facilities. Types of establishment range from the most sumptuous kind of 'Grand Hotel' to the trendiest imaginable sort of designer experience to rustic chalets. Room rates, which normally include an excellent breakfast, vary according to the time of year; mountain resorts are more expensive during the winter sports season, Salzburg and other centres during festival times, and Vienna during the summer and over Christmas and New Year. But Austria generally offers excellent value compared with many other European countries.

In high season it is advisable to book accommodation in advance, though local tourist offices will almost always be able to help you find a room somewhere. Some hotels, especially in rural areas away from the ski resorts, close for a couple of months over the winter. Naturally, rates are lower in winter than in summer, though the reverse can be true where skiing is the main attraction.

A number of brochures are available from the Austrian National Tourist Office. Two give details of hundreds of one- to three-star and three- to five-star hotels respectively. A *Kinderhotels* brochure describes dozens of independent establishments providing high quality accommodation and facilities for families and there is also a website, www.kinderhotels.co.uk. A selection of spa hotels is illustrated in a *Spa Austria* brochure, and again there is a useful website, www.spa.austria.info.

Alternatives to hotels include staying on a farm *(Ferien im Bau-ernhof)*, renting an apartment *(Ferienwohnung)*, dossing down in a mountain hut *(Hütte)*, or using campsites and youth hostels. More than 3,000 farms take in guests, many of them providing healthy meals made from their own organic produce. The website www.farmholidays.com gives information. Renting an apartment *(Ferienwohnung)* is likely to be an economic way of managing a longer stay for those preferring a degree of independence, while a walking holiday using mountain huts will be an exhilarating experience.

Do you have a single room/ double room?	**Haben Sie ein Einzelzimmer/ ein Doppelzimmer?**
What does the room cost?	**Was kostet das Zimmer?**

AIRPORTS *(Flughafen)*

The busiest and best-equipped airport in Austria is **Wien-Schwechat** (VIE, www.viennaairport.com), about 20km (12 miles) southeast of central Vienna. The airport is connected to the centre of Vienna by rail and motorway. The quickest connection (16 minutes) is by the modern CAT (City Airport Train; €10) which runs half-hourly to and from the City Air Terminal at Wien-Mitte station from around 6am–midnight. A much cheaper and slightly slower (25-minute) connection is provided by S-Bahn *(Schnellbahn* or rapid transit; €3.60) to the same destination. Airport buses (from €7) run to and from Vienna's mainline rail stations (Südbahnhof and Westbahnhof) and Schweden-platz/Morzinplatz in the city centre. A taxi to central Vienna should cost around €35.

An alternative airport for travellers to Vienna is the international airport serving Bratislava in Slovakia, which is linked to Schwechat (65km/40 miles away) and the city centre by express buses.

The airports at Graz (GRZ), Innsbruck (INN), Klagenfurt

(KLU), Linz (Blue Danube; LNZ) and Salzburg (W.A. Mozart; SZG) are served by a comparatively limited number of international flights. Destinations in southern Carinthia are only an hour's drive from the international airports at Ljubljana and Maribor in Slovenia, while the international airport at Zürich in Switzerland (and to a lesser extent, Friedrichshafen airport in Germany) are convenient for Bregenz and Vorarlberg. Northern Tyrol can be reached from the major international airport at Munich in Germany.

Where can I find a taxi?	**Wo finde ich ein Taxi?**
How much is it to the centre?	**Wieviel kostet es ins Zentrum?**
Does this bus go to the railway station?	**Fährt dieser Bus zum Bahnhof?**

B

BICYCLE HIRE *(Fahrradverleih)*

Bicycles can be hired from cycle shops in most towns and resorts. Austrian Railways (ÖBB) offer bikes for hire from around 120 stations, at half the normal rate if you have begun your journey by rail (normal rates are around €20 per day). This scheme has the advantage that the bike can be left at a station other than the one you have hired it from. Your own bicycle can be carried in the luggage compartment of trains. Find information on cycle routes at www.radtouren.at (see also page 130).

BUDGETING FOR YOUR TRIP

Prices in Austria generally correspond with the European average, though in some respects the country is noticeably less expensive than its neighbours Switzerland and Germany. The quality of goods and services is high, and most visitors feel they get good value for money.

Accommodation. Double room in three-star hotel in Vienna: €130–200; four-star hotel: €200–250. Prices are lower in the provinces.

Bars. Expect to pay between €3 and €4 for a half litre of beer and about the same for a glass of wine or a shot of spirits. Non-alcoholic drinks start at around €1.50 for a glass of mineral water. Tap water isn't normally served and probably won't come free if it is.

Entertainment. Cinema from around €8 (reductions on certain days), nightclub around €40, disco from €5, theatre, concert or opera from €12 (standing from €5).

Flights. In July and August expect to pay between £150 and £200 on flag carrier airlines from the UK. Prices are lower in winter.

Meals. A two-course meal ordered from the *Tageskarte* can cost as little as €6 in a simple inn or restaurant, while a gourmet meal with wine at a sophisticated establishment will cost upwards of €40.

Sightseeing. Entrance fees to museums vary from around €5–10. Many museums grant free admission on certain days or at certain times, and there are reductions for children and students. Holders of a 'Vienna Card' are entitled to reductions, and similar cards are available for other cities and whole provinces.

Public transport. Rail travel is not particularly expensive; a single second-class ticket between Vienna and Innsbruck (527km/328 miles) costs around €58, and less for children, students and people over 60. An InterRail Austria Pass giving unlimited travel for three non-consecutive days within a 15-day period costs around €150, and similar passes are available for four, six and eight days. Most cities offer a 'Card' giving unlimited use of public transport for a specified period as well as free or reduced admission to many attractions; the 'Vienna Card', valid for 72 hours, costs €19.90. Taxis normally have meters; a minimum fee of €2.50 or more is usually charged, plus a fee per kilometre of around €1.20.

C

CAMPING AND CARAVANNING

There are plenty of well-regulated and maintained campsites all over Austria, mainly in popular holiday areas where they often enjoy highly scenic locations, but even in Vienna (Camping Wien; www.wiencamping.at; three sites) and Salzburg (Camping Nord Sam; www.camping-nord-sam.com). Most sites have a good range of facilities. Camping or parking a caravan at the roadside or without the landowner's permission is not allowed. To find a campsite in the area where you want to stay, log on to the website www.campsite.at.

CAR HIRE *(Autovermietung)* (see also Driving)

The major international car-hire companies operate in Austria, with desks at airports, in city centres and at some main railway stations. Daily/weekly rates start at around €60/260.

To hire a car you will normally need to be over 21 and to have held a valid driving licence for over a year. An International Driving Permit is not required for visitors from EU countries, Canada and the USA. Insurance is compulsory and it is prudent to take out full cover. No cash deposit is required if paying by credit card. Rental vehicles should display a motorway vignette.

Car hire companies In Austria include: Europcar (tel: 866 16 10; www.europcar.at), Avis (tel: 1 70 073 2700; www.avis.at), Budget (tel: 1 70 073 2700 ; www.budget.at), Easymotion (tel: 664 857 7000; www.easymotion.at) and Hertz (tel: 1 70 073 2661; www.hertz.at).

CLIMATE

Austria has a basically temperate climate, though there are significant regional differences and altitude plays a decisive role. Summers are warm, with the highest temperatures in the lower Danube valley and south of the Alps, where temperatures can reach 30°C (86°F) or more. Occasional showers, sometimes heavy, are likely. At high altitudes, snow can fall at any time of the year, and climbers and walkers must expect rapid changes in conditions. Winters are cold, with temperatures descending to -6°C (21°F) in low-lying areas, often accompanied by fog, rain and snow. From November to March there are likely to be heavy snowfalls in the Alps, with temperatures dropping to -10°C (14°F) and lower, though south of the main ridge there may be plenty of sunshine.

CLOTHING

Even in summer, evenings can be cool, especially in the Alps, so be sure to take along something warm as well as a waterproof outer garment. A jacket or coat is advisable for spring and autumn. Cold winters make a warm coat, gloves and headgear essential. Robust weatherproof clothing and sturdy hiking boots are essential for mountain walking. Austrians like to dress up for the theatre and opera, though a dark suit/cocktail dress will be sufficient for all but the most formal occasions.

CRIME AND SAFETY

Austria is a rather convention-bound society and the level of crime, though rising, is less than in some comparable countries. Nevertheless, all the usual precautions should be taken. You should have some sort of ID on you at all times, and it is a good idea to make a photocopy of your passport and have a record of the numbers of your credit and other cards. Report thefts and incidents to the police (*Polizei*) who are generally very helpful to visitors from Western countries.

D

DRIVING

To drive your own car in Austria you will need a valid driving licence, vehicle insurance certificate, registration document, national identity sticker and red breakdown triangle. The headlights of right-hand drive cars must be fitted with a beam converter kit. To drive on motorways and similar roads you must purchase and display a *Vignette* (sticker), available from filling stations, post offices and tobacconists, and at frontier crossings. These cost €7.90 for 10 days, €23 for two months and €76.50 for a year. Additional tolls are payable for use of certain sections of road such as the Brenner autobahn.

Road conditions. Traffic can be heavy, particularly during the morning and evening rush hours, and at the beginning and end of holiday periods, partly because of Austria's role as a transit country between northern and southern Europe. In winter, it may be advisable to fit winter tyres or chains, and many pass routes are closed. There is a useful car shuttle train service between Böckstein in Salzburger Land and Mallnitz in Carinthia through the Tauern rail tunnel.

Rules and regulations. Drive on the right and give way to traffic coming from the right unless on a road identified by a yellow diamond priority sign. Give way to passengers boarding or alighting from a tram and to people on foot at pedestrian crossings and when turning right. There are severe penalties for drinking and driving; the alcohol limit is set at 0.049 percent, meaning that you are at risk after a single drink. Seat belts must be worn and children under 12 must have a safety seat. Headlights must be used in low visibility and parking lights illuminated on unlit roads. Mobile telephones may not be used while driving. Speed limits unless otherwise indicated: motorways 130kmh (81mph); other roads 100kmh (62mph); built-up areas 50kmh (31mph). A high-visibility vest must be carried in the car.

Disregard of rules and regulations can lead to the police levying heavy on-the-spot fines.

Parking. Parking is regulated in the centres of towns and cities. It may be free of charge, but time-limited, in which case a parking disc must be obtained and set (available from tobacconists). Elsewhere, on-street parking is controlled by means of vouchers or meters.

Breakdowns and assistance. The warning triangle must be displayed to indicate a broken-down vehicle and hazard lights must be switched on. Assistance can be obtained by calling the ÖAMTC (Austrian Automobile Club), tel: 120, or ARBÖ (Austrian Drivers' Association), tel: 123. Accidents involving injury must be reported to the police.

Road signs. These are generally the same as in the rest of Europe. Frequently used written signs include:

Ausfahrt	Exit
Baustelle	Roadworks
Einbahnstrasse	One-way street
Ende	End
Fahrbahnwechsel	Change lanes
Fussgänger	Pedestrians
Glatteis	Icy surface
Langsam	Slow
Rollsplit	Loose gravel
Steinschlag	Falling stones
Umleitung	Diversion
Vorsicht!	Take care!

E

ELECTRICITY

Electricity is supplied at 230 volts/50 herz. Sockets take standard European two-pin plugs; British and American appliances need adaptors.

EMBASSIES AND CONSULATES

Contact your country's embassy if you lose your passport, have trouble with the authorities or suffer an accident.

Australia: Mattiellistrasse 2–4, 1040 Vienna; tel: 01 506 740; www.austria.embassy.gov.au

Canada: Laurenzberg 2, 1010 Vienna; tel: 01 531 383 000; www.canadainternational.gc.ca

Ireland: Rotenturmstrasse 16–18, 1010 Vienna; tel: 01 715 4246; www.embassyofireland.at

New Zealand: Mattiellistrasse 2–4, 1040 Vienna; tel: 01 505 3021; www.nzembassy.com/austria

South Africa: Sandgasse 33, 1190 Vienna; tel: 01 320 6493; www.dirco.gov.za/vienna/

United Kingdom: Jauresgasse 12, 1030 Vienna; tel: 01 716 130; http://ukinaustria.fco.gov.uk

United States: Boltzmanngasse 16, 1090 Vienna; tel: 01 313 390; http://austria.usembassy.gov/

Where is the British Embassy?	**Wo ist die britische Botschaft?**

EMERGENCIES

In an emergency the pan-European emergency number **120** should be called. The old numbers for the various emergency services also still work.

Police **133**

Fire **122**

Ambulance **144**

Fire!	**Feuer!**
Help!	**Hilfe!**
Police	**Polizei**
Hospital	**Spital**
Doctor	**Arzt**

G

GAY AND LESBIAN TRAVELLERS

As might be expected, attitudes to gayness differ widely between Vienna and the provinces. The capital has plenty of gay-friendly bars and other establishments, and in June stages an annual gay festival, *Wien Andersrum* (Vienna the Other Way Round), which is brought to a close by a Rainbow Parade along the Ring. The Life Ball, which takes place in May and was founded as an Aids awareness event, is one of the more glittering events of the ball season. A 'Vienna Queer Guide' is available for download from the city's tourism website, www.vienna.info. There are also smaller-scale gay scenes in Linz, Innsbruck, Salzburg and Graz. In the countryside, while overt hostility is unlikely, attitudes are much more conservative.

GETTING THERE

By Air. The national carrier, Austrian Airlines (www.aua.com), operates frequent flights from most European capitals and many major cities to the country's main international hub, Vienna-Schwechat, and less frequent ones to the airports at Graz, Innsbruck, Klagenfurt, Linz and Salzburg. There are also direct Austrian flights to Schwechat from New York, Atlanta and Tokyo.

Many other carriers, including the major national operators and some budget airlines, connect Schwechat with European destinations, while all intercontinental destinations can be reached with a change of plane in Zürich, Frankfurt or London.

The provincial airports are served by fewer operators. The following details of flights from the UK and Ireland are liable to change.
Graz: London Stansted (Ryanair).
Innsbruck: London Gatwick (EasyJet); Bristol (EasyJet); Liverpool (EasyJet).
Klagenfurt: London Stansted (Ryanair).
Linz: London Stansted (Ryanair).

Salzburg: London Gatwick (British Airways, EasyJet); London Stansted (Ryanair); Manchester (British Airways); Bristol, Liverpool, Luton (EasyJet), Edinburgh, Leeds/Bradford, Manchester (Jet2).

Budget operators also serve other destinations in the UK and in Ireland, though not necessarily all year round, and there are budget and other flights to airports in countries outside Austria (such as Bratislava and Munich) which are nevertheless convenient for certain Austrian destinations (see Airports).

By rail. The national rail company (*Österreichische Bundesbahnen* – ÖBB, Austrian Federal Railways; www.oebb.at) operates comfortable and reliable international services in cooperation with the railways of neighbouring countries. There are direct links from Germany, Switzerland, Italy, and several Eastern European countries. Travel to Austria by rail from Britain takes between 16 and 18 hours and involves at least two changes and, although various reduced-price tickets are available, is likely to cost more than a comparable flight. However, it is certainly an option worth considering if you wish to visit other destinations on the way and fancy a bit of railway romance. From London St Pancras there are two routes: via Paris and Munich and via Brussels, Cologne and Frankfurt. For information, see www.raileurope.co.uk and www.seat61.com.

By Road. (See also Driving.) Austria is linked to all its neighbours by motorways or good main roads. Vienna is about 1,300km (800 miles) from the car-ferry port of Calais in France with its frequent sailings to and from Dover. The French terminal of the Channel Tunnel with its car-shuttle service is also at Calais. The best route to Vienna is via Belgium and Germany and is entirely on toll-free motorways (though remember that a Vignette must be purchased in order to drive on motorways in Austria). Klagenfurt in Carinthia is a slightly longer drive from Calais, while Bregenz at the western tip of Austria is about 860km (535 miles) if French motorways are used, in which case tolls will amount to around €50.

The burden of driving can be eased by taking an overnight Auto im Reisezug (Motorail) service from Düsseldorf in Germany to Salzburg, Innsbruck or Villach. There are also internal Motorail services including useful links from Feldkirch in Vorarlberg to Vienna, Graz, and to Villach in Carinthia. For information and to book, see the Austrian Railways website, www.oebb.at. Vienna and other Austrian cities are connected to London by coach services, with trips taking upwards of 20 hours. Fares to Vienna start at £73. Log on to www. eurolines.co.uk for information and to book online.

GUIDES AND TOURS

Tourist information and marketing services are well developed and English-speaking guides are available in most places. If a live commentary is only in German there is likely to be a handout in English, and audio guides are often available in an English version. Local tourist information centres are a mine of information. Walking tours of cities, often with a theme (eg Mozart's Salzburg, The Third Man tour in Vienna), are a fascinating alternative to the more conventional bus tour. A trot around the centre of Vienna in a traditional *Fiaker* (horse-drawn cab) can be fun, though agree a price beforehand. Steamer trips on the many lakes or on the Danube are a relaxed way of taking in the scenery.

Reputable tour companies Include: Vienna City Tours (tel: 01 311 52 37; www.viennacitytours.com) and Salzburg Panorama Tours (tel: 0662 88 32 110; www.panoramatours.com).

HEALTH AND MEDICAL CARE

No special precautions need to be taken when travelling to Austria, which is generally a very safe, clean and healthy country with excellent medical services. Emergency medical care is free of charge for EU citizens, though you may have to pay for medicines. Before travelling, British subjects should obtain a free European Health

Insurance Card (forms available at post offices, online at www.ehic. org.uk, or tel: 0845 606 2030). Citizens of countries outside the EU should ensure that they are covered by a comprehensive private health insurance policy. Such insurance is worth considering in any case in order to cover any longer-term problems and to ensure prompt repatriation if necessary. Minor health problems can often be dealt with by visiting a pharmacy *(Apotheke)*. These sport a green cross and/or snake and staff sign. In big cities several stay open all night and the addresses should be posted in the windows of those that close. In Vienna go to www.wien-vienna.com/nachtapotheken. php for a list of all-night pharmacies. In case of accident or serious illness, call the ambulance service on **144** or general emergency number **120**.

L

LANGUAGE

Austrians speak German, albeit with an accent very different from standard High German. English is widely spoken and understood, particularly by people in the tourism and hospitality industry, but it is polite not to assume this and to enquire *Sprechen Sie englisch?* before plunging ahead. Slovene is spoken by a tiny minority in southern Carinthia and Hungarian and Croatian by similar numbers in parts of Burgenland.

M

MAPS *(Karten)*

The local maps and town plans supplied free by tourist information centres, car-hire firms and some hotels and banks may be all that you need for a short stay. Superior town plans are published by the local firm of Freytag & Berndt (www.freytagberndt.at), who are also responsible for excellent walking and cycling maps and for a series of road atlases including the commendably helpful Strassen & Städte Österreich – Europa (Roads and Towns Austria – Europe) with large-scale town plans and maps of the whole country at 1:150,000 scale.

MEDIA

English-language newspapers such as The *Guardian*, the *Daily Mail*, the *International Herald Tribune*, and *USA Today* can be found at kiosks in the major towns and resorts, sometimes with a day's delay. There is also the online *Austria Today*, though its full content is only available by subscription. Perhaps surprisingly, Austria has no equivalent of the magisterial German or Swiss dailies like the *Frankfurter Allgemeine Zeitung* or *Neue Zürcher Zeitung*. The most reputable dailies are the right-of-centre *Die Presse* and the more left-leaning *Der Standard*, though neither is as wide-reaching as the populist tabloid *Kronen Zeitung*. Full cultural listings are published in Vienna's monthly *Monatsprogramm*.

Most hotels have satellite or cable TV providing one or more English-language channels such as BBC World News or CNN. The principal local channels are ORF1 and ORF2.

MONEY (Geld)

The euro (€) is the official currency used in Austria. Notes are denominated in 5, 10, 20, 50, 100 and 500 euros (last two rarely seen); coins in 1 and 2 euros and 1, 2, 5, 10, 20 and 50 cents.

May I pay with this credit card?	**Kann ich mit dieser Kreditkarte bezahlen?**
I want to change some pounds/dollars.	**Ich möchte Pfund/Dollar wechseln.**
Where is the nearest cash machine/bank/ bureau de change?	**Wo ist der nächste Geldautomat/die nächste Bank/Wechselstube?**

Changing money. The easiest way to obtain euros is with a suitable debit/credit card at a cash machine *(Geldautomat)*, but note that not all cards are accepted at all machines and that most banks charge for this service. Foreign currency can be changed at practically any bank or savings bank *(Sparkasse)*. As well as bureaux de change, travel agencies and hotels will often change money, though the rate is not likely to be a favourable one.

Credit cards. Cash still rules in Austria, but you should be able to settle your hotel bill using your credit/debit card. Occasionally you may come across an establishment that only takes one type of card.

O

OPENING HOURS

Banks. Monday to Friday 8am–3pm, possibly with later opening on Thursday.

Museums. Most museums open at 9am or 10am and close at 5pm or 6pm, though there may be late opening on one day a week. Many are closed all day Monday. See individual listings in the Where to Go section.

Shops. Official opening hours are Monday to Friday 9am–6pm with early closing on Saturday. Small shops close at lunch time while larger establishments may open earlier and stay open longer one evening a week.

P

POLICE *(Polizei)*

Previously consisting of municipal forces and a national *Gendarmerie*, Austria's *Bundespolizei* (Federal Police) is now a unified organisation. Uniforms, vehicles and signs are all a combination of dark blue, silver and red. Officers are generally polite and helpful and some speak English. To summon the police call **133** or the general emergency number **120**. The main police station in Vienna is at Schottenring 7–9, in Salzburg at Alpenstrasse 88–99.

Where is the nearest police station?	**Wo ist die nächste Polizeiwachstube?**

POST OFFICES *(Postamt)*

Post offices offer the usual range of services. Opening hours are normally Mon–Fri 8am–6pm but larger cities have one or more offices open around the clock, sometimes in the main railway station, though not all services may be available at night. Letterboxes and post office signs are coloured yellow. Stamps can also be bought at tobacconists *(Tabaktrafik)* and sometimes at places that sell postcards.

Where is the nearest post office?	**Wo ist das nächste Postamt?**
Airmail	**Luftpost**
Express (special delivery)	**Per Express/Eilbote**
Registered	**Per Einschreiben**

PUBLIC HOLIDAYS *(Feiertage)*

1 January	**Neujahr**	New Year's Day
6 January	**Dreikönigstag**	Epiphany
March/April	**Ostermontag**	Easter Monday
1 May	**Tag der Arbeit**	May Day/Labour Day
May/June	**Christi Himmelfahrt**	Ascension Day
May/June	**Pfingstmontag**	Whit Monday
June	**Fronleichnam**	Corpus Christi
15 August	**Mariä Himmelfahrt**	Assumption Day
26 October	**Nationalfeiertag**	National Day
1 November	**Allerheiligen**	All Saints Day

8 December	**Maria Empfägnis**	Immaculate Conception
25 December	**Weihnachtsfeiertag**	Christmas Day
26 December	**Weihnachtsfeiertag (2)**	St Stephen's Day

T

TELEPHONE

Local SIM cards are inexpensive and as Austria is a member of the EU, roaming charges are low. Rather than cash, most public telephones take phonecards, available from post offices and tobacconists.

To call Austria from abroad, dial 00 43 followed by the area code (minus the 0) and the number. To make an international call from Austria, dial 00 followed by the country code, area code and number. Within Austria, to make a call from one city to another dial the relevant area code starting with zero, then the subscriber number. You do not need the area code when dialling within the same city/code area.

TIME ZONE

Austria follows Central European Time (GMT +1 hour) and in summer an hour is added for daylight saving.

Auckland	Sydney	Jo'burg	**Vienna**	London	New York
10pm	8pm	noon	**noon**	11am	6am

TIPPING

Although a service charge is included in restaurant bills, it is customary to round the amount up to the nearest euro or round figure. A small sum is also expected by cloakroom attendants, porters, chambermaids and tour guides.

TOILETS

Well-maintained public toilets can usually be found in town centres and railway stations. Keep small change handy in case there is a charge. Men's toilets are marked with the word 'Herren', Ladies with 'Damen'.

TOURIST INFORMATION

The Austrian National Tourist Office (ANTO) dispenses comprehensive information on the internet and in brochure form about where to go, what to see and where to stay and dine. Visit the website at www.austria.info.

Brochures can be ordered from the following ANTO offices:

Australia: 1st floor, 36 Carrington Street, Sydney, NSW 2000; tel: +61 (2) 9299 3621.

Ireland: tel: 189 0930118.

UK: 3rd floor, 9–11 Richmond Buildings, London W1D 3HF; tel: +44 (0) 20 7440 3848.

USA: PO Box 1142, New York, NY 10108-1142; tel: +1 (212) 944 68 80.

The following is a list of tourist offices in Austria's main visitor hotspots:

Vienna: Albertinaplatz 1010; tel: 01 24 555; www.wien.info.

Salzburg: Mozartplatz 5, other branches at the main railway station, airport and southern park & ride; tel: 0662 889 873 30; www.salzburg.info.

Innsbruck: Burggraben 3; tel: 0512 535 60; www.innsbruck.info.

Graz: Herrengasse 16; tel: 0316 807 50; www.graztourismus.at.

Klagenfurt: Neuer Platz 1; tel: 0463 537 2223; www.info.klagenfurt.at.

TRANSPORT *(Öffentlicher Verkehr)*

Air. Domestic flights between Vienna and Graz, Linz, Salzburg, Innsbruck and Klagenfurt are operated by Austrian Airlines.

Rail. Given the comfortable, clean and reliable services operated by ÖBB and a small number of private companies, rail is the preferred method of travel for many journeys within Austria. The almost completely electrified network is comprehensive, reaching virtually every town and major resort, leaving only smaller places and remote villages to be served by bus.

Types of train include fast (but not ultra high-speed) Eurocity (EC) and InterCity (IC) linking the main centres. Vienna to Linz takes around 1.5 hours, Salzburg around 2.5 hours, Innsbruck around 5 hours and Bregenz around 7.5 hours. First-class accommodation is luxurious, second-class comfortable. If there is no dining car, a mobile buffet service is available. There are also compartments reserved for women and play facilities for children on some trains. Most services run at regular intervals (hourly or two-hourly) and the system is highly integrated, with convenient connections to local trains and bus services.

Local and regional trains, including those operated by private companies, are marginally less fast and comfortable, but equally reliable. The Greater Vienna area is served by an extensive *S-Bahn* (suburban rail) network with fast trains running at 15- or 30-minute intervals.

Fares are comparable with or slightly less expensive than those of neighbouring countries and are calculated by kilometre, with reductions for students, senior citizens etc. There are many special offers which can be checked on the *ÖBB* website, www.oebb.at. They include various cards/passes giving unlimited travel over the whole or parts of the network for specified periods. Among them are travel cards for use of all forms of public transport – rail, bus, boats, cable cars etc. – in a particular area, though in the case of mountain railways they may only entitle the user to a reduction in the normal fare.

City transport. Getting around Austria's major cities is made easy by the existence of fully integrated transport systems, based mainly on buses, but also (in Linz, Graz and Innsbruck) on trams, and in Vienna on the five U-Bahn (underground) and several S-Bahn (*Schnellbahn* or rapid transit) lines as well as the 30 tramlines.

Single tickets are available, but it is invariably cheaper to buy books of tickets or 24-hour or longer passes, available from ticket machines or tobacconists.

Bus. Anywhere not served by rail will have a bus service, usually operated by the reliable *ÖBB* postbuses. Times of services are often designed to suit commuters and children going to and from school, and there may be no service on Sundays. Tickets can be bought from the driver, though again if you are making more than the occasional trip it will be worth investigating what cards and passes are available locally.

Many ski resorts have a free shuttle service serving the various slopes. Given the excellent rail network, intercity bus services are less developed than in some countries, though there is a fast ÖBB bus link between Graz and Klagenfurt.

Mountain transport. Most visitors to Austria will want to experience the effortless ascent of one or more mountains by means of cable car *(Seilbahn)*, gondola *(Gondelbahn)*, chair-lift *(Sesselbahn)* or rack-and-pinion railway *(Zahnradbahn)*. Fares can be quite expensive, though reductions can invariably be obtained by buying local and regional cards and passes.

VISAS AND ENTRY REQUIREMENTS

A valid passport or identity card (for most EU citizens) is necessary for entry into Austria. There is no visa requirement for visitors from nearly all Western countries.

WEBSITES AND INTERNET ACCESS

Wi-fi is available at most hotels of any standard but is not free as often as it is in the UK. If you are taking your laptop along, consider purchasing a cheap local 'dongle' plug-in to access the internet anywhere there is a mobile phone signal. These can cost as little as €20. Useful websites:

www.tiscover.at An alternative to the official tourist information website.

www.aboutaustria.org General information on Austria and the Austrians.

www.austrianews.co.uk Up-to-date news from Austria.

www.austria.org The website of the Austrian Embassy in the USA, full of information about the country, including news updates.

www.austriatoday.at Daily coverage of Austrian politics, business, culture, sports and general news.

Y

YOUTH HOSTELS

There are around 100 well-run youth hostels in Austria, with accommodation ranging from basic (dormitories) to quite plush (choice of room sizes). Check sites like www.hostelworld.com or www.hostel-bookers.com or seek more information from the *Österreichischer Jugendherbergsverband* (Austrian Youth Hostels Association), 1010 Vienna, Schottenring 28, tel: 01 5333 53 53, www.oejhv.or.at. Below is a list of recommended hostels:

Schloßherberge am Wilhelminenberg Savoyenstrasse 2, Vienna; tel: 01 481 0300; shb@hostel.at; dorm beds from €24.

Jugendherberge Wien Myrthengasse Myrthengasse 7, Vienna: tel: 01 523 6316; hostel@chello.at; dorm beds from €17.

Eduard Heinrich Haus Eduard-Heinrich-Strasse 2, Salzburg: tel: 0662 625 976; heinrichhaus@hostel-salzburg.at; dorm beds from €21.

Jugendherberge Innsbruck Reichenauer Strasse 147, Innsbruck; tel: 0512 346 179; info@youth-hostel-innsbruck.at; dorm beds from €21.

Jugendherberge Universitätsviertel Neckheimgasse 6, Klagenfurt: tel: 0463 230 020; jgh.klagenfurt@oejhv.or.at; dorm beds from €21.

Recommended Hotels

The following hotels in towns, cities and regions throughout Austria are listed under the major headings used in the Where to Go section. A number of luxury establishments are included, but the emphasis is on mid-range places to stay which are particularly characteristic of the country or local area or which have some special feature. Advance booking is recommended, especially in summer and, in popular skiing resorts, during the winter sports season, when rates are also at their highest. Prices also rise during festival time in cities such as Salzburg and Bregenz. It is always worthwhile investigating special deals.

As a basic guide to prices for a double room with breakfast the following symbols are used:

€€€€   over 200 euros
€€€   150–200 euros
€€   100–150 euros
€   under 100 euros

VIENNA

Altstadt Vienna €€–€€€ *A-1070 Wien, Kirchengasse 41, tel: 01 522 66 66,* www.hotelamstephansplatz.at. Housed in a 19th-century apartment block, attentive staff, cutting edge decor and a location within walking distance of most sights make this a sure-fire winner. Room rates include breakfast and afternoon tea, a feature you won't find in many other places. Rooms are in converted apartments with tall windows, double doors and preposterously high ceilings.

Das Triest €€€€ *A-1040 Wien, Wiedner Hauptstrasse 12, tel: 01 589 180,* www.dastriest.at. Once the starting point for the stagecoach service to the port of Trieste on the Adriatic, this establishment was transformed into the city's first designer hotel by Terence Conran, and has all the stylish features you would expect. The restaurant looks out on to the courtyard garden.

Das Tyrol €€€ *A-1060 Wien, Mariahilfer Strasse 15, tel: 01 587 54 15,* www.dastyrol.at. Located in the MuseumsQuartier, this boutique hotel has brightly decorated rooms, pristine bathrooms and a breakfast you'll be looking forward to the night before. The hotel is littered with pieces of contemporary art to get you in the mood for Vienna's many museums and galleries.

Hotel Am Stephansplatz €€€ A-1010 Wien, Stephansplatz 9, tel: 01 534 050, www.altstadt.at. Right at the heart of the city, this much-lauded hotel a few steps from the Stephansdom offers 56 comfortable rooms with wood floors and elegantly understated furnishings. Choice at breakfast is vast and you can admire views of the cathedral from the breakfast room windows as you eat.

Imperial €€€€ A-1015 Wien, Kärtner Ring 16, tel: 01 500 100, www. luxurycollection.com/imperial. This sumptuous palace was built as his private Vienna residence by the Prince of Württemberg in 1863 and converted into the city's leading hotel 10 years later. Favoured by royals, statesmen and pop stars, it has lavishly furnished and decorated public spaces and rooms and suites with every comfort (even butler service). *Echt* (authentic) Viennese café and gourmet restaurant.

König von Ungarn €€€€ A-1010 Wien, Schulerstrasse 10, tel: 01 515 84, www.kvu.at. A stone's throw from St Stephen's Cathedral, the 400-year-old 'King of Hungary' is a city institution, much favoured in the past by Magyar aristocrats. Its attractive rooms are all individually furnished. The atrium with a tree growing up through it is a special feature.

Pension Pertschy €€ A-1010 Wien, Habsburgergasse 5, tel: 01 534 490, www.pertschy.com. Old-fashioned, friendly pension on several floors of a Baroque palace with a galleried courtyard. The location just off Graben could not be more central.

Zipser €–€€ A-1080 Wien, Lange Gasse 49, tel: 01 404 540, www. zipser.at. In a rather grand, century-old building, this attractive pension has been run with great care by the same family for three generations. Rooms facing the garden are slightly more expensive. Just beyond the Ring in the interesting Josefstadt district, a few minutes' walk from the *Rathaus* and the Inner City.

LOWER AUSTRIA

Althof €€ *A-2070 Retz, Althofgasse 14, tel: 02942 3711,* www.althof.at. The venerable 'city castle' of this old wine town, one of the jewels of the Weinviertel, is now a comfortable hotel with spacious, contemporary rooms. Stylish restaurant overlooking one of the courtyards, plus a vaulted vinotheque.

Loisium Wine and Spa Resort €€€ *A-3550 Langenlois, Loisium Allee 2, tel: 02734 77100 0,* www.loisiumhotel.at. The innovative Loisium, contemporary symbol of Austria's largest wine town, is complemented by this lavish hotel and spa, from American architect Steven Holl.

Romantik Hotel Richard Löwenherz €€€–€€€€ *A-3601 Dürnstein 8, tel: 02711 222,* www.richardloewenherz.at. There is no more romantic spot along the Danube than tiny Dürnstein, and no more romantic place to stay there than in the aptly named Romantic Hotel Richard Lionheart. Atmospherically fitted into the buildings of a 13th-century convent, the hotel has spacious, beautifully furnished rooms; some, like the restaurant, overlook the river.

Schloss Dürnstein €€€€ *A-3601 Dürnstein 2, tel: 02711 212,* www. schloss.at. Even more characterful than the Richard Lionheart above, this little Renaissance castle is furnished with valuable antiques and offers luxurious accommodation, indoor and outdoor pools and a vaulted restaurant above the Danube.

BURGENLAND

Das Schmidt €€ *A-7072, Mörbisch am See, Raffeisenstrasse 8, tel: 02685 82 94,* www.das-schmidt.at. In a lakeside village famous for its floating stage, this large and stylish family-run establishment has a 'Roman-Pannonian' wellness centre and natural mud baths. Some rooms with balconies and lake views.

Romantik-Purbachhof € *A-7083 Purbach am Neusiedlersee, Schulgasse 14, tel: 02683 55 64.* By the church in the tiny wine-growing town of Purbach, this delightful 16th-century building with its sunny courtyard was once the residence of a Hungarian vintner. Sensitively restored and modernised, it offers a warm welcome and a choice of 10 rooms. Closed Nov–Apr.

Rusterhof €€ *A-7071 Rust, Rathausplatz 18, tel: 02685 607 93, www. hotelbuergerhaus-rust.at.* On the main square in the Neusiedlersee's prettiest town, this Baroque mansion is famous for its cuisine but also has lovely, individually furnished bedrooms and more expensive suites.

STYRIA

Brauhaus Mariazell €€–€€€ *A-8630 Mariazell, Wienerstrasse 5, tel: 03882 252 30, www.bierundbett.at.* With only a couple of characterful bedrooms, accommodation in this historic brewery just round the corner from Mariazell's pilgrimage basilica needs to be booked well in advance, but is worth the effort.

Gasthof-Pension Zur Steirerstub'n € *A-8020 Graz, Lendplatz 8, tel: 0316 716 855, www.pension-graz.at.* A budget choice in Styria's capital city, this friendly *Gasthof* has simply furnished rooms with showers. There are views of the city's Schlossberg hill with its clock tower, and the centre is only a few minutes' walk away on the far bank of the River Mur. Restaurant with local specialities.

Joseph €€ *A-8461 Sulztal an der Weinstrasse 13, tel: 03453 4575, www. joseph-hotel.com.* A converted farmhouse located among vineyards, Joseph is one of the most attractive and welcoming places to stay in the region known as 'Styrian Tuscany'. Mediterranean-style restaurant, landscaped garden and heated pool.

Posthotel €€–€€€ *A-8970 Schladming, Hauptplatz 10, tel: 03687 225 71, www.alte-post.at.* The most atmospheric place to stay in the busy resort of Schladming is this venerable, family-run hotel on the main square. Pleasant, traditionally furnished bedrooms, restaurant, and rustic panelled *Stube*.

Schlossberg €€–€€€ *A-8010 Graz, Kaiser-Franz-Josef-Kai 30, tel: 0316 807 00, www.schlossberg-hotel.at.* This elegant 16th-century town mansion is a few steps from the middle of Graz. Tastefully furnished, restful interiors, and an all-pervasive air of restrained luxury, plus a swimming pool high among the rooftops.

CARINTHIA AND EAST TYROL

Buchenhof €–€€ *A-9220 Velden, Sternbergstrasse 40, tel: 04274 43 43,* www.buchenhof.at. In rustic surroundings high above the resort of Velden on the Wörthersee, this friendly guesthouse run by Hildegard and Bruno Mitterberger is a budget alternative to the more expensive lakeshore establishments.

Haus Senger €€ *A-9844 Heiligenblut, Hof 23, tel: 04824 22 15,* www.romantic.at. The Alpine village of Heiligenblut guarding the southern approach to the Grossglockner has nowhere more authentic to stay than this comfortable chalet hotel, grown out of an old farmstead.

Inselhotel €€ *A-9583 Faak am See, Inselweg 10, tel: 04254 21 45,* www.inselhotel.at. This establishment on its own little island in Lake Faaker can only be reached by hotel motorboat. Contemporary rooms, most with superb views, plenty of leisure facilities and restaurant with terrace.

Kleinsasserhof €–€€ *A-9800 Spittal an der Drau, Kleinsass 3, tel: 04762 22 92,* www.kleinsasserhof.at. This rustic guesthouse, high up among the meadows a short distance from the town of Spittal, offers its guests an intriguing philosophy of life as well as a warm welcome and solid food from fresh ingredients. Simple, attractive, individually furnished rooms.

Parkhotel Tristachersee €€€ *A-9900 Lienz, Tristachersee 1, tel: 04852 676 66,* www.parkhotel-tristachersee.at. Just outside East Tyrol's little capital, Lienz, this immaculately run hotel has a tranquil lake shore location backed by woodland. There is attentive service, a new wellness centre, and fine dining (half-board) is included in the room rate.

Romantik-Hotel Post €€ *A-9500 Villach, Hauptplatz 26, tel: 04242 26 10 10,* www.romantik-hotel.com. Kings, queens and emperors have ruffled the sheets at this aristocratic mansion on Villach's main square, which retains many period features and offers comfortable accommodation plus a much-lauded restaurant.

Schloss Velden €€€€ *A-9220 Velden, Schlosspark 1, tel: 04274 520 0000, www.falkensteiner.com.* This imposing lakeside establishment in the swish Wörthersee resort of Velden looks back on centuries of history and achieved great fame in the German-speaking world as the setting of a TV soap opera. Now completely refurbished, it offers every conceivable luxury, albeit at some expense.

UPPER AUSTRIA

Gasthof Zum Goldenen Schiff € *A-4470 Enns, Hauptplatz 23, tel: 07223 860 86, www.hotel-brunner.at.* On the main square of exquisite little Enns, claimed to be Austria's oldest town, this family-run guesthouse offers individually furnished, attractively renovated rooms.

Hotel Deim – Gasthof zum Goldenen Hirschen €€ *A-4240 Freistadt, Böhmergasse 8, tel: 07842 722 580, www.hotels-freistadt.at.* In the heart of the unspoiled Mühlviertel, not far from the Czech border, medieval Freistadt offers no more atmospheric place to stay than this comfortable and well-run old inn, whose origins go back to the 13th century.

Romantic Hotel Minichmayr €€ *A-4400 Steyr, Haratzmüllerstrasse 1, tel: 07252 534 10, www.hotel-minichmayr.com.* Overlooking the confluence of two rivers, this 500-year-old building is the best-located hotel in historic Steyr. Many of the comfortable and carefully modernised rooms have commanding views over the water to the picturesque silhouette of the old town.

Wolfinger €–€€ *A-4020 Linz, Hauptplatz 19, tel: 070 773 29 10, www.hotelwolfinger.at.* This historic hotel on Linz's main square welcomed its first guests in the early 17th century. Vaulted interiors and pleasantly modernised rooms, some furnished with antique pieces.

SALZKAMMERGUT

Goldenes Schiff €€–€€€ *A-4820 Bad Ischl, Adalbert-Stifler-Kai 3, tel: 06132 242 41, www.goldenes-schiff.at.* With gastronomic traditions going back hundreds of years, and run by the same family for three generations, the 'Golden Ship' stands on the banks of the River Traun. The hotel has an attractive, contemporary ambience, and all bedrooms are tastefully contemporary.

Im Weissen Rössl €€€ *A-5360 Sankt Wolfgang im Salzkammergut, Markt 74, tel: 06138 230 60, www.weissesroessl.at.* The 100-year-old 'White Horse' owes its fame not only to its starring role in a famous operetta, but also to its comfort, traditional ambience, high quality service and lakeside location – one of the best in the Salzkammergut.

SALZBURG AND SALZBURGER LAND

Arthotel Blaue Gans €€€–€€€€ *A-5020 Salzburg, Getreidegasse 41, tel: 0662 84 24 91 50, www.hotel-blaue-gans-salzburg.at.* Resolutely rejecting the 'designer' label, this rather exquisite establishment nevertheless provides unobtrusive luxury and soothing decor. It also offers excellent value, given its location at one end of Salzburg's pedestrianised main thoroughfare, the Getreidegasse.

Bloberger Hof €–€€ *A-5020 Salzburg, Hammerauerstrasse 4, tel: 0662 830 227, www.blobergerhof.at.* A short bus ride from central Salzburg, this is the sort of homely, family-run guesthouse you won't want to leave. Wonderful mountain views and outstanding food.

Goldener Hirsch €€€–€€€€ *A-5020 Salzburg, Getreidegasse 37, tel: 0662 808 40, www.goldenerhirsch.com.* Salzburg's most famous hotel, the 'Golden Stag' has been accommodating visitors for over six centuries. Consisting of three cleverly integrated town mansions and an annexe, it is in the very heart of the city. The decor combines luxury with traditional touches such as hunting trophies.

Romantic Hotel Zell am See €€–€€€ *A-5700 Zell am See, Sebastian-Hörl-Strasse 11, tel: 06542 725 20, www.romantic-hotel.at.* This traditional timber chalet in the centre of Zell am See has comfortable, contemporary interiors and is laid out around its indoor and outdoor pool, heated in winter. Guests can also use the lakeside beach nearby.

Gasthof Eggerwirt €€ *A-6370 Kitzbühel, Untere Gänsbachgasse 12, tel: 05356 624 55*, www.eggerwirt-kitzbuehel.at. Just outside the centre of the glamorous ski resort, this delightful old inn has a history of hospitality going back centuries and has been in the same family for generations. Welcoming, comfy and good value in an expensive location.

Goldener Adler €€–€€€ *A-6020 Innsbruck, Herzog-Friedrich-Strasse 6, tel: 0512 711 111*, www.goldeneradler.at. Innsbruck's most historic place to stay, the 'Golden Eagle' is a buttressed, arcaded medieval building in the heart of the Altstadt. Guests have included Mozart and Goethe.

Ritzlerhof €€–€€€ *A-6432 Sautens im Ötztal, tel: 05252 626 80*, www.ritzlerhof.at. In an idyllic location high above the Ötztal, one of Austria's loveliest Alpine valleys, this modern chalet-type, family-run establishment offers comfortable rooms and an extraordinary array of recreational facilities. It's a 15-minute walk to the Piburgersee, Tyrol's warmest bathing lake.

Deuring-Schlössle €€€€ *A-6900 Bregenz, Ehre-Guta-Platz 4, tel: 05574 478 00*, www.deuring-schloessle.at. The most atmospheric place to stay in Bregenz, this 600-year-old castle in the charming Upper Town has luxurious, individually furnished rooms. Aristocratic ambience and marvellous views over town and Lake Constance. Gourmet restaurant.

Gams €€€ *A-6870 Bezau, Platz 44, tel: 05514 22 20*, www.hotel-gams.at. One of the prettiest villages of the Bregenzerwald, Bezau boasts this extraordinary establishment, a traditional *Gasthof* with an ultra-modern extension guaranteed to pamper its guests in every way and ideal for romantic breaks.

INDEX

Achensee 113
Altausseer See 94
Archäologischer Park
    Magdalensberg 77
Arlberg 118
Attersee 91

Bad Aussee 94
Bad Blumau 68
Baden 49
Badgastein 102
Bad Gleichenberg 67
Bad Ischl 89
    Kaiservilla 90
Bad Radkersburg 67
Bärnbach 66
Bregenz 121
    Kunsthaus Bregenz 122
    Oberstadt 122
    Pfander 123
    Seebuhne 122
    Vorarlberger
        Landesmuseum 122
Bregenzerwald 123
Brenner Pass 110
Bruck an der Mur 68
Burg Aggstein 57
Burg Hochosterwitz 77

Carnuntum 51

Dachstein 71
Dürnstein 56

Ebensee 92
Eggenburg 54

Osterreichisches Mo-
    torradmuseum 54
Ehrenhausen 67
Eisenstadt
    Bergkirche 59
    Burg Forchenstein 59
    Haydnhaus 59
    Schloss Esterházy 59
Eisriesenwelt 101
Enns 87

Faakersee 80
Feldkirch 124
Friesach 79
Fuchs Palast 78

Galtür 119
Gamlitz 67
Gesäuse gorge 70
Gmünd 81
Gmunden 92
Graz 61
    Burg 62
    Domkirche 63
    Hauptplatz 62
    Kunsthaus Graz 64
    Landhaus 62
    Murinsel 64
    Rathaus 62
    Schlossberg 63
    Schloss Eggenberg 64
    Zeughaus 62
Grossglockner Hochal-
    penstrasse 82
Grundlsee 94
Gurk 79

Hainburg 51
Hall 111
Hallein 100
Hallstatt 92
    Dachstein Caves 94
    Krippenstein 94
    Mammuthöhle 94
    Museum 93
    Salzwelten Hallstatt 93
Hallstatter See 92
Hardegg 53
Heiligenblut 82
Hintertux 115
Hochgurgl 118
Hohenwerfen 101
Hunerkogel 71
Hüttenberg 79

Igls 110
Innsbruck 106
    Domkirche 108
    Ferdinandeum 108
    Goldenes Dachl 107
    Grabmal Kaiser Maxi-
        milians I 108
    Hofkirche 108
    Hungerbergbahn 109
    Museum Goldenes
        Dachl 108
    Schloss Ambras 110
    Stadtturm 108
    Tiroler Volkskunst-
        museum 108
    Triumphpforte 107
    Zeughaus 109
Ischgl 119

Kaiser-Franz-Josephs-
　　Hohe 105
Kammersee 95
Kaprun 102
Kaunertal 118
Kitzbühel 112
Klagenfurt 72
　　Alter Platz 74
　　Hauptpfarrkirche St
　　　Egid 74
　　Landesmuseum 74
　　Minimundus 75
　　Neuer Platz 73
Klosterneuburg
　　Stift Klosterneuburg 47
Krems 55
Kremsmünster 86
Krimmler Wasserfälle 105
Kufstein 112

Lake Constance 120
Lake Erlauf 69
Landeck 119
Langenlois 56
Lech 120
Leoben 69
Liechtensteinklamm 101
Lienz 83
Linz 84
　　Ars Electronica Center
　　　85
　　Hauptplatz 85
　　Lentos Kunstmu-
　　　seum 85
　　Postlingberg 86
Lipizzaner Welt Piber 65

Malta-Hochalm-Strasse 82
Marchfeld 50

Maria Alm am Steinernen
　　Meer 104
Maria Saal 77
Maria Wörth 77
Mariazell 69
Maurach 114
Mayrhofen 115
Millstätter See 81
Mondsee 91
Mühlviertel 88

Obergurgl 118
Ossiacher See 80
Ötztal 117

Percholdsdorf 48
Piburger See 117
Pinzgau 102
Pitztal 118
Pörtschach 76

Ramsau 71
Retz 53
Riegersburg 68
Rohrau 52

Saalbach 102
Salzburg 96
　　Dom 97
　　Getreidegasse 97
　　Hohensalzburg 98
　　Kapuzinerberg 99
　　Mozarts Geburtshaus
　　　97
　　Mozart-Wohnhaus 99
　　Peterskirche 98
　　Residenz 97
　　Schloss Hellbrunn 99
　　Schloss Mirabell 99

Salzwelten Altaussee 95
Salzwelten Salzburg 101
Samnaun 119
Schladming 71
Schloss Artstetten 58
Schloss Riegersburg 54
Seefeld 115
Seewinkl 60
Silvretta-Hochalpenstrasse
　　125
Sölden 117
Spittal an der Drau 81
St Christoph am Arlberg
　　119
Steinernes Meer 103
Steyr 87
St Gilgen 91
Stift Admont 71
Stift Altenburg 54
Stift Melk 57
St Johann im Pongau 101
St Johann in Tirol 112
Stubing 65

Traunsee 92

Velden 76
Vienna 29
　　Akademie der bil-
　　　denden Künste 40
　　Albertina 35
　　Alte Burg 33
　　Augustinerkirche 35
　　Belvedere 43
　　Burggarten 32
　　Burgtheater 39
　　Heergeschichtliches
　　　Museum 45
　　Hofburg 32

Hundertwasserhaus 45
Jüdisches Museum 31
Karlskirche 41
Kunsthistorisches Museum 36
Leopold Museum 38
MAK 43
Mozarthaus 31
MUMOK 38
Naschmarkt 42
Naturhistorisches Museum 37
Neue Burg 33
Neues Rathaus 39
Parlament 40

Peterskirche 31
Prater 45
Prunksaal 35
Schloss Schönbrunn 46
Secessionsgebäude 40
Sissimuseum 34
Spanish Riding School 35
Staatsoper 31
Stadtpark 42
Stephansdom 30
Stephansplatz 29
Votivkirche 40
Wien Museum Karlsplatz 41

Villach 79

Wachau 55
Waldviertel 53
Weinviertel 52
Wienerwald 48
Wolfgangsee 90
Wörthersee 75

Zell-am-See 102
Zell am Ziller 114
Zillertal 114
Zugspitze 116
Zürs 120
Zwölferhorn 90

Berlitz pocket guide

Austria

Second Edition 2012
Reprinted 2013

Written by Mike Ivory
Updated by Marc Di Duca
Commissioned by Rebecca Lovell
Picture Researcher: Lucy Johnston
Series Editor: Tom Stainer
Production: Tynan Dean, Linton Donaldson and Rebeka Ellam

Photography credits
Fotolia 1; Britta Jaschinski 2TL, 53, 143; Austrian National Tourist Office 2TR, 2M, 3TL, 3TR, 3MR, 3BL, 3BR, 4All, 5All, 6All, 7T, 7B, 8, 10, 12, 21, 28, 31, 34, 35, 37, 38, 39, 41, 43, 44, 45, 47, 48, 49, 51, 52, 53, 54, 59, 60, 65, 68, 69, 70, 72, 74, 75, 76, 78, 79, 80, 82, 84, 87, 88, 89, 90, 91, 93, 94, 95, 96, 97, 99, 100, 101, 103, 104, 105, 106, 107, 108, 110, 113, 114, 116, 119, 120, 122, 123, 124, 125, 128, 129, 131, 133, 134, 135, 136, 138, 141, 144, 146; iStockphoto 2B, 13, 56, 58, 63, 66, 67; Wolfgang Fritz 3ML; akg-images London 7M, 32; Augsburg City Archive 16; Corbis 19, 22, 83; Wilhelm Klein 20
Cover Picture: 4Corners Images

Every effort has been made to provide accurate information in this publication, but changes are inevitable. The publisher cannot be responsible for any resulting loss, inconvenience or injury.

Contact us

At Berlitz we strive to keep our guides as accurate and up to date as possible, but if you find anything that has changed, or if you have any suggestions on ways to improve this guide, then we would be delighted to hear from you.

Berlitz Publishing, PO Box 7910, London SE1 1WE, England.
email: berlitz@apaguide.co.uk
www.insightguides.com/berlitz

Berlitz®

speaking your language

phrase book & dictionary
phrase book & CD

Available in: Arabic, Cantonese Chinese, Croatian, Czech, Danish, Dutch, English*, Finnish*, French, German, Greek, Hebrew*, Hindi, Hungarian*, Indonesian, Italian, Japanese, Korean, Latin American Spanish, Mandarin Chinese, Mexican Spanish, Norwegian, Polish, Portuguese, Romanian*, Russian, Spanish, Swedish, Thai, Turkish, Vietnamese

*Book only